# ACCUPLACER MATH SUCCESS

# SECOND EDITION

## with Math Concept and Formula Review Study Guide

## INCLUDES

## 200 ACCUPLACER MATH PROBLEMS AND SOLUTIONS

# TABLE OF CONTENTS

**Part 1 – Math Concept and Formula Review Study Guide**

**Arithmetic concepts:**

Computations with Integers     2

Fractions: Multiplying Fractions     4

         Dividing Fractions     5

         Finding the Lowest Common Denominator (LCD)     6

         Simplifying Fractions     8

Mixed Numbers     10

PEMDAS – Order of Operations     12

Percentages and Decimals     15

Practical Problems     16

Setting Up Basic Equations     18

Working with Estimates     20

**Algebra concepts and formulas:**

Absolute Value     23

Combinations and Permutations     24

The FOIL Method and Working with Polynomials

         Multiplying Polynomials Using the FOIL Method     26

         Dividing Polynomials Using Long Division     27

         Substituting Values in Polynomial Expressions     28

         Operations on Polynomials Containing Three Terms     29

Factoring Polynomials

         Basic Factoring     30

         Factoring – Advanced Problems     31

         Factoring to Find Possible Values of a Variable     35

Fractions Containing Fractions     36

Fractions Containing Radicals     38

Fractions Containing Rational Expressions

     Adding and Subtracting Fractions Containing Rational Expressions     39

     Multiplying Fractions Containing Rational Expressions     40

     Dividing Fractions Containing Rational Expressions     42

Imaginary and Complex Numbers     44

Inequalities     44

Laws of Exponents

     Adding and Subtracting Exponents     48

     Fractions as Exponents     50

     Negative Exponents     51

     Zero Exponent     51

Logarithmic Functions     52

Matrices     53

Multiple Solutions     54

Scientific Notation     56

Sequences and Series

     Arithmetic Sequences and Series     56

     Geometric Sequences and Series     58

Sigma Notation     59

Solving by Elimination     61

Solving for an Unknown Variable     62

Special Operations     63

Square Roots, Cube Roots, and Other Radicals

     Factoring Radicals     65

Multiplication of Radicals     67

Rationalizing Radicals     68

Systems of Equations     69

**Geometry concepts and formulas:**

Angle Measurement     72

Arcs     73

Area     74

Circumference     77

Diameter     78

Distance Formula     79

Hypotenuse Length     80

Midpoints     82

Perimeter of Squares and Rectangles     84

Radians     85

Slope and Slope-Intercept     86

Volume     88

$x$ and $y$ intercepts     89

**Trigonometry concepts and formulas:**

Angles     93

Cosine     94

Sine     96

Tangent     98

**ACCUPLACER MATH PRACTICE**

Arithmetic and Algebra Problems     100

College-Level Algebra and College-Level Math Problems     106

# STEP-BY-STEP SOLUTIONS

Solutions to the Arithmetic and Algebra Problems     117

Solutions to the Algebra Problems     148

# MATH CONCEPT AND FORMULA REVIEW STUDY GUIDE

**Arithmetic concepts:**

The arithmetic part of the Accuplacer Test will have questions on the following:

- Computations with Integers

- Basic Operations with Fractions

- Basic Operations with Mixed Numbers

- Exponent Laws

- Order of Operations

- Percentages and Decimals

- Practical Problems

- Setting Up Basic Equations

- Square Roots (Radicals)

- Working with Estimates

Advanced questions on square roots, fractions, and exponents will be covered on the algebra part of the test.

We provide examples for each of the above topics in this pre-algebra section, apart from square roots and exponents, which we have included in the algebra section.

## Computations with Integers

Computations with integers are extremely common on the Accuplacer examination.

Integers are positive and negative whole numbers. Integers cannot have decimals, nor can they be mixed numbers. In other words, they can't contain fractions.

One of the most important concepts to remember about integers is that two negative signs together make a positive number.

Why do two negatives make a positive? In plain English, you can think of it like using "not" two times in one sentence.

For example, you tell your friend: "I do not want you to not go to the party."

In the sentence above, you are really telling your friend that you want him or her to attend the party.

In other words, the "two negatives" concept in math is similar to the "two negatives" concept in the English language.

So, when you see a number like $-(-2)$ you have to use 2 in your calculation.

Look at the example problem that follows.

Problem 1:

$-(-5) + 3 = ?$

A.  $-8$

B.  $-2$

C.  2

D.  5

E.  8

The correct answer is E.

According to the concepts stated above, we know that $-(-5) = 5$

So, we can substitute this into the equation in order to solve it.

$- (-5) + 3 = ?$

$5 + 3 = 8$

**A+**  Remember that when you see two negatives signs together, you need to make a positive number.

You will also see problems that ask you to perform multiplication or division on integers.

Some of these problems may ask you to find an integer that meets certain mathematical requirements, like in problem 2 below.

Problem 2:

What is the largest possible product of two even integers whose sum is 22?

A.  11

B.  44

C. 100

D. 120

E. 144

The correct answer is D.

For problems that ask you to find the largest possible product of two even integers, first you need to divide the sum by 2.

The sum in this problem is 22, so we need to divide this by 2.

$22 \div 2 = 11$

Now take the result from this division and find the 2 nearest even integers that are 1 number higher and lower.

$11 + 1 = 12$

$11 - 1 = 10$

Then multiply these two numbers together in order to get the product.

$12 \times 10 = 120$

**Fractions – Multiplying**

You will see problems on the exam that ask you to multiply fractions.

 When multiplying fractions, multiply the numerators from each fraction. Then multiply the denominators.

The numerator is the number of the top of each fraction.

The denominator is the number on the bottom of the fraction.

Problem:

What is $^1/_3$ × $^2/_3$?

A. $^2/_3$

B. $^2/_6$

C. $^2/_9$

D. $^1/_3$

E. $^1/_6$

The correct answer is C.

Multiply the numerators.

1 × 2 = 2

Then multiply the denominators.

3 × 3 = 9

These numbers form the new fraction.

$^2/_9$

**Fractions – Dividing**

You will also need to know how to divide fractions for the exam.

 A+ | To divide fractions, invert the second fraction by putting the denominator on the top and numerator on the bottom. Then multiply.

Problem:

$$\frac{1}{5} \div \frac{4}{7} = ?$$

A. $\dfrac{4}{20}$

B. $\dfrac{7}{20}$

C. $\dfrac{4}{35}$

D. $\dfrac{5}{35}$

E. $\dfrac{7}{35}$

The correct answer is B.

Remember to invert the second fraction by putting the denominator on the top and the numerator on the bottom.

Our problem was: $\dfrac{1}{5} \div \dfrac{4}{7} = ?$

So the second fraction $\dfrac{4}{7}$ becomes $\dfrac{7}{4}$ when inverted.

Now use the inverted fraction to solve the problem.

$$\frac{1}{5} \div \frac{4}{7} =$$

$$\frac{1}{5} \times \frac{7}{4} = \frac{7}{20}$$

## Fractions – Finding the Lowest Common Denominator (LCD)

In some fraction problems, you will have to find the lowest common denominator.

In other words, before you add or subtract fractions, you have to change them so that the bottom numbers in each fraction are the same.

You do this my multiplying the numerator [top number] by the same number you use on the denominator for each fraction.

 A+ | Remember to multiply the numerator and denominator by the same number when you are converting to the LCD.

Problem:

What is $\frac{1}{9} + \frac{9}{27}$?

A. $\frac{12}{27}$

B. $\frac{9}{27}$

C. $\frac{3}{27}$

D. $\frac{10}{36}$

E. $\frac{5}{9}$

The correct answer is A.

STEP 1: To find the LCD, you have to look at the factors for each denominator.

Factors are the numbers that equal a product when they are multiplied by each other.

So, the factors of 9 are:

1 × 9 = 9

3 × 3 = 9

The factors of 27 are:

1 × 27 = 27

3 × 9 = 27

STEP 2: Determine which factors are common to both denominators by comparing the lists of factors.

In this problem, the factors of 3 and 9 are common to the denominators of both fractions.

We can illustrate the common factors as shown below.

We saw that the factors of 9 were:

1 × **9** = 9

**3** × 3 = 9

The factors of 27 were:

1 × 27 = 27

**3** × **9** = 27

So, the numbers in bold above are the common factors.

STEP 3: Multiply the common factors to get the lowest common denominator.

The numbers that are in bold above are then used to calculate the lowest common denominator.

3 × 9 = 27

So, the lowest common denominator (LCD) for each fraction above is 27.

STEP 4: Covert the denominator of each fraction to the LCD.

You convert the fraction by referring to the factors from step 3.

Multiply the numerator and the denominator by the same factor.

7

Our problem was $\frac{1}{9} + \frac{9}{27} = ?$

So, we convert the first fraction as follows:

$$\frac{1}{9} \times \frac{3}{3} = \frac{3}{27}$$

We do not need to convert the second fraction of $\frac{9}{27}$ because it already has the LCD.

STEP 5: When both fractions have the same denominator, you can perform the operation to solve the problem.

$$\frac{1}{9} + \frac{9}{27} =$$

$$\frac{3}{27} + \frac{9}{27} = \frac{12}{27}$$

**Fractions – Simplifying**

You will also need to know how to simplify fractions.

A+ | To simplify fractions, look to see what factors are common to both the numerator and denominator.

In the example problem above, our result was $\frac{12}{27}$.

Problem:

Simplify: $\frac{12}{27}$

A. $\frac{1}{3}$

B. $\frac{3}{4}$

C. $\frac{3}{9}$

D. $\dfrac{4}{9}$

E. $\dfrac{5}{9}$

The correct answer is D.

STEP 1: Look at the factors of the numerator and denominator.

The factors of 12 are:

1 × 12 = 12

2 × 6 = 12

**3** × 4 = 12

You will remember that the factors of 27 are:

1 × 27 = 27

**3** × 9 = 27

So, we can see that the numerator and denominator have the common factor of 3.

STEP 2: Simplify the fraction by dividing the numerator and denominator by the common factor.

Our fraction in this problem is $\dfrac{12}{27}$.

So, simplify the numerator: 12 ÷ 3 = 4

Then simplify the denominator: 27 ÷ 3 = 9

STEP 3: Use the results from step 2 to form the new fraction.

The numerator from step 2 is 4.

The denominator is 9.

So, the new fraction is $\dfrac{4}{9}$.

## Mixed Numbers

Mixed numbers are those that contain a whole number and a fraction.

 Convert the mixed numbers back to fractions first. Then find the lowest common denominator of the fractions in order to solve the problem.

Problem:

$$3\frac{1}{3} - 2\frac{1}{2} = ?$$

A. $\dfrac{1}{3}$

B. $\dfrac{9}{3}$

C. $\dfrac{5}{6}$

D. $1\frac{1}{2}$

E. $1\frac{1}{6}$

The correct answer is C.

Our problem was: $3\dfrac{1}{3} - 2\dfrac{1}{2} = ?$

STEP 1: Convert the first mixed number to an integer plus a fraction.

$3\frac{1}{3} =$

$3 + \dfrac{1}{3}$

STEP 2: Then multiply the integer by a fraction whose numerator and denominator are the same as the denominator of the existing fraction.

$$3 + \frac{1}{3} =$$

$$\left(3 \times \frac{3}{3}\right) + \frac{1}{3} =$$

$$\frac{9}{3} + \frac{1}{3}$$

STEP 3: Add the two fractions to get your new fraction.

$$\frac{9}{3} + \frac{1}{3} = \frac{10}{3}$$

Then convert the second mixed number to a fraction, using the same steps that we have just completed for the first mixed number.

$$2\tfrac{1}{2} =$$

$$2 + \frac{1}{2} =$$

$$\left(2 \times \frac{2}{2}\right) + \frac{1}{2} =$$

$$\frac{4}{2} + \frac{1}{2} = \frac{5}{2}$$

Now that you have converted both mixed numbers to fractions, find the lowest common denominator and subtract to solve.

$$\frac{10}{3} - \frac{5}{2} =$$

$$\left(\frac{10}{3} \times \frac{2}{2}\right) - \left(\frac{5}{2} \times \frac{3}{3}\right) =$$

$$\frac{20}{6} - \frac{15}{6} =$$

$$\frac{5}{6}$$

**PEMDAS – Order of Operations**

The phrase "order of operations" means that you need to know which mathematical operation to do first when you are faced with longer problems.

Remember the acronym PEMDAS. "PEMDAS" means that you have to do the mathematical operations in this order:

First: Do operations inside **P**arentheses

Second: Do operations with **E**xponents

Third: Perform **M**ultiplication and **D**ivision (from left to right)

Last: Do **A**ddition and **S**ubtraction (from left to right)

Some students prefer to remember the order or operations by using the memorable phrase:

## Please Excuse My Dear Aunt Sally

Refer to the rules above and attempt the example problems that follow.

Problem 1:

$-6 \times 3 - 4 \div 2 = ?$

A.  −20

B.  −18

C.  −2

D.  4

E.  3

The correct answer is A.

There are no parentheses or exponents in this problem, so we need to direct our attention to the multiplication and division first.

Our problem was: $-6 \times 3 - 4 \div 2 = ?$

When you see a problem like this one, you need to do the multiplication and division from left to right.

This means that you take the number to the left of the multiplication or division symbol and multiply or divide that number on the left by the number on the right of the symbol.

So, in our problem we need to multiply $-6$ by 3 and then divide 4 by 2.

You can see the order of operations more clearly if you put in parenthesis to group the numbers together.

$-6 \times 3 - 4 \div 2 =$

$(-6 \times 3) - (4 \div 2) =$

$-18 - 2 = -20$

Now try a problem that has parenthesis, exponents, multiplication, division, addition, and subtraction.

Problem 2:

$$\frac{5 \times (7-4)^2 + 3 \times 8}{5 - 6 \div (4-1)} = ?$$

A.  $-23$

B.  $23$

C.  $\dfrac{23}{\frac{1}{3}}$

D.  $128$

E.  $346.67$

The correct answer is B.

For this type of problem, do the operations inside the **parentheses** first.

$$\frac{5 \times (7-4)^2 + 3 \times 8}{5 - 6 \div (4-1)} =$$

$$\frac{5 \times (3)^2 + 3 \times 8}{5 - 6 \div 3}$$

Then do the operation on the **exponent**.

$$\frac{5 \times (3)^2 + 3 \times 8}{5 - 6 \div 3} =$$

$$\frac{5 \times (3 \times 3) + 3 \times 8}{5 - 6 \div 3}$$

$$\frac{5 \times 9 + 3 \times 8}{5 - 6 \div 3}$$

Then do the **multiplication** and **division**.

$$\frac{5 \times 9 + 3 \times 8}{5 - 6 \div 3} =$$

$$\frac{(5 \times 9) + (3 \times 8)}{5 - (6 \div 3)} =$$

$$\frac{45 + 24}{5 - 2}$$

Then do the **addition** and **subtraction**.

$$\frac{45 + 24}{5 - 2} = \frac{69}{3}$$

In this case, we can then simplify the fraction since both the numerator and denominator are divisible by 3.

$$\frac{69}{3} = 69 \div 3 = 23$$

## Percentages and Decimals

You will have to calculate percentages and decimals on the exam, as well as use percentages and decimals to solve other types of math problems or to create equations.

Percentages can be expressed by using the symbol %. They can also be expressed as fractions or decimals.

In general, there are three ways to express percentages.

TYPE 1:  Percentages as fractions

Percentages can always be expressed as the number over one hundred.

So 45% = $\frac{45}{100}$

TYPE 2:  Percentages as simplified fractions

Percentages can also be expressed as simplified fractions.

In order to simplify the fraction, you have to find the largest number that will go into both the numerator and denominator.

In the case of 45%, the fraction is $\frac{45}{100}$, and the numerator and denominator are both divisible by 5.

To simplify the numerator: 45 ÷ 5 = 9.

To simplify the denominator: 100 ÷ 5 = 20.

This results in the simplified fraction of $\frac{9}{20}$.

TYPE 3:  Percentages as decimals

Percentages can also be expressed as decimals.

45% = $\frac{45}{100}$ = 45 ÷ 100 = 0.45

You may have to use these concepts in order to solve a practical problem, like the one that follows.

Problem:

Consider a class which has $n$ students. In this class, $t\%$ of the students subscribe to digital TV packages.

Which of the following equations represents the number of students who do not subscribe to any digital TV package?

A. $100(n - t)$

B. $(100\% - t\%) \times n$

C. $(100\% - t\%) \div n$

D. $(1 - t)n$

E. $n - t$

The correct answer is B.

If $t\%$ subscribe to digital TV packages, then $100\% - t\%$ do not subscribe.

In other words, since a percentage is any given number out of 100%, the percentage of students who do not subscribe is represented by this equation:

$(100\% - t\%)$

This equation is then multiplied by the total number of students ($n$) in order to determine the number of students who do not subscribe to digital TV packages.

$(100\% - t\%) \times n$

**Practical Problems**

Several questions on the Accuplacer Test will ask you to solve practical problems.

Practical problems may involve calculating a discount on an item in a store. Other common practical problems involve calculations with exam scores or other data for a class of students.

Now have a look at another type of practical problem, which involves knowledge of basic equations.

We will look at basic equations in more depth in the "Setting Up Basic Equations" section of this study guide.

For some basic equation problems, you will see two equations which the have the same two variables, like $J$ and $T$ in the problem below.

Problem:

A company sells jeans and T-shirts. $J$ represents jeans and $T$ represents T-shirts in the equations below.

$2J + T = \$50$

$J + 2T = \$40$

Sarah buys one pair of jeans and one T-shirt. How much does she pay for her entire purchase?

A. $10

B. $20

C. $30

D. $70

E. $90

The correct answer is C.

In order to solve the problem, take the second equation and isolate $J$ on one side of the equation. By doing this, you define variable $J$ in terms of variable $T$.

$J + 2T = \$40$

$J + 2T - 2T = \$40 - 2T$

$J = \$40 - 2T$

Now substitute $\$40 - 2T$ for variable $J$ in the first equation to solve for variable $T$.

$2J + T = 50$

$2(40 - 2T) + T = 50$

$80 - 4T + T = 50$

$80 - 3T = 50$

$80 - 3T + 3T = 50 + 3T$

$80 = 50 + 3T$

$80 - 50 = 50 - 50 + 3T$

$30 = 3T$

$30 \div 3 = 3T \div 3$

$10 = T$

So, now that we know that a T-shirt costs $10, we can substitute this value in one of the equations in order to find the value for the jeans, which is variable $J$.

$2J + T = 50$

$2J + 10 = 50$

$2J + 10 - 10 = 50 - 10$

$2J = 40$

$2J \div 2 = 40 \div 2$

$J = 20$

Now solve for Sarah's purchase. If she purchased one pair of jeans and one T-shirt, then she paid:

$10 + $20 = $30

**Setting Up Basic Equations**

You will see problems on the test that ask you to make mathematical equations from basic information.

To set up an equation, read the problem carefully and then express the facts in terms of an algebraic equation.

These types of questions are often practical problems that involve buying or selling merchandise.

Problem 1:

A company purchases cell phones at a cost of $x$ and sells the cell phones at four times the cost.

Which of the following represents the profit made on each cell phone?

A. $x$

B. $3x$

C. $4x$

D. $3 - x$

E. $4 - x$

The correct answer is B.

The sales price of each cell phone is four times the cost.

The cost is expressed as $x$, so the sales price is $4x$.

The difference between the sales price of each cell phone and the cost of each cell phone is the profit.

REMEMBER: Sales Price − Cost = Profit

In this problem, the sales price is $4x$ and the cost is $x$.

$4x - x = $ Profit

$3x = $ Profit

Problem 2:

An internet provider sells internet packages based on monthly rates. The price for the internet service depends on the speed of the internet connection. The chart that follows indicates the prices of the various internet packages.

| Price in dollars ($P$) | 10 | 20 | 30 | 40 |
|---|---|---|---|---|
| Gigabyte speed ($s$) | 2 | 4 | 6 | 8 |

Which equation represents the prices of these internet packages?

A. $P = (s - 5) \times 5$

B. $P = (s + 5) \times 5$

C. $P = 5 \div s$

D. $P = s \times 5$

E. $P = s \div 5$

The correct answer is D.

The price of the internet connection is always 5 times more than the speed.

$10 = 2 \times 5$

$20 = 4 \times 5$

$30 = 6 \times 5$

$40 = 8 \times 5$

So, the price of the internet connection (represented by variable $P$) equals the speed (represented by variable $s$) times 5.

$P = s \times 5$

**Working with Estimates**

You will see questions on the arithmetic part of the test that ask you to estimate the result of multiplying or diving two numbers.

For estimation problems, round the numbers up or down. Then perform the operation.

Problem:

Estimate the result of the following: 6.2 × 3.9 = ?

A. 10

B. 18

C. 24

D. 48

E. 54

The correct answer is C.

STEP 1: Round the numbers up or down.

6.2 becomes 6.

3.9 becomes 4.

STEP 2: Then perform the operation.

6 × 4 = 24

## Algebra concepts and formulas:

The algebra and college algebra parts of the exam cover:

- absolute value
- combinations and permutations
- the FOIL method and other operations with polynomials
- factoring polynomial expressions
- fractions containing rational and radical expressions
- imaginary and complex numbers
- inequalities
- laws of exponents
- logarithmic functions
- matrices
- multiple solutions
- scientific notation
- sequences and series
- sigma notation
- solving problems by substitution and elimination
- solving problems for an unknown variable
- special operations
- square roots
- systems of equations

You may also see some coordinate geometry problems in the algebra section of the test. That is because you need to use algebraic concepts to solve certain coordinate geometry problems.

Advanced coordinate geometry problems and plane geometry are included in the college-level math part of the exam.

**Absolute value**

A+

When you see numbers between lines like this | $x$ |, you are being asked the absolute value. Absolute value measures the distance of a number from zero, so absolute value is always a positive number.

Problem:

| 5 – 8 | = ?

A. –3

B. –5

C. –8

D. 3

E. 5

The correct answer is D.

Absolute value is always a positive number.

| 5 – 8 | = – | –3 |

| –3 | = 3

Note that if there is a negative sign in front of the absolute value, you have to make the absolute value negative.

For example:

– | 8 – 10 | =

– | –2 | =

–2

**Combinations and permutations:**

A+

To determine the number of combinations of $S$ at a time that can be made from a set containing $N$ items, you need this formula: $(N!) \div [(N - S)! \times S!]$

Problem 1 – Combinations:

How many 2 letter combinations can be made from the following set?: M N P Q

A. 4

B. 6

C. 7

D. 8

E. 9

The correct answer is B.

Remember that to determine the number of combinations of $S$ at a time that can be made from a set containing $N$ items, you need this formula: $(N!) \div [(N - S)! \times S!]$

In the question above, $S = 2$ (because you are combining the letters two at a time) and $N = 4$ (because there are four letters in the set).

The ! symbol means that you have to multiply the given number by all of the positive integers that are less than it, as shown in the example below.

Now substitute the values for $S$ and $N$:

$(4 \times 3 \times 2 \times 1) \div [(4 - 2)! \times (2!)] =$

$(4 \times 3 \times 2) \div [2 \times 1) \times (2 \times 1)] =$

$24 \div 4 = 6$

So, 6 two-letter combinations can be made from a four letter set.

Question 2 – Permutations:

A+

To determine the number of permutations of $S$ at a time that can be made from a set containing $N$ items, you need this formula:

$N! \div (N - S)!$

How many 3 letter permutations can be made from this character set?:   &  £  #  @

A. 10

B. 12

C. 14

D. 20

E. 24

The correct answer is E.

Remember that to determine the number of permutations of $S$ at a time that can be made from a set containing $N$ items, you need this formula:  $N! \div (N - S)!$

Unlike combinations, permutations take into account the order of the items in each possible set.

For example, A B C and C A B are different permutations.

For the question above, $N = 4$ and $S = 3$.

Solve the question as follows:

$N! \div (N - S)! =$

$(4 \times 3 \times 2 \times 1) \div (4 - 3)! =$

$(4 \times 3 \times 2 \times 1) \div 1 =$

$24 \div 1 = 24$

**The FOIL Method and Working with Polynomials**

Polynomials are algebraic expressions that contain integers, variables, and variables which are raised to whole-number positive exponents.

You will certainly see problems involving polynomials on the Accuplacer Test. Be sure that you know these concepts well.

*Multiplying Polynomials Using the FOIL Method:*

The use of the FOIL method is one of the most important things you will need to know in order to answer many of the algebra questions on the test.

You will see many problems in this format on the test: $(x + y)(x + y)$.
Use the FOIL method to solve these problems, multiplying the terms in the parentheses in this order: First – Outside – Inside – Last

Look at the example algebra question below on the FOIL method. Note that there are several other problems covering this skill in the practice problems that follow this part of the study guide.

Problem:

$(3x - 2y)^2 = ?$

A. $9x^2 + 4y^2$

B. $9x^2 - 6xy^2 + 4y^2$

C. $9x^2 - 12xy^2 + 4y^2$

D. $9x^2 + 12xy^2 + 4y^2$

E. $9x^2 + 12xy^2 - 4y^2$

The correct answer is C.

When you see algebra questions like this one, use the FOIL method.

Study the solution below, which highlights the order to carry out the operations on the terms.

$(3x - 2y)^2 = (3x - 2y)(3x - 2y)$

FIRST: The first terms in each set of parentheses are $3x$ and $3x$: $(\mathbf{3x} - 2y)(\mathbf{3x} - 2y)$

$3x \times 3x = 9x^2$

OUTSIDE: The terms on the outside are $3x$ and $-2y$: $(\mathbf{3x} - 2y)(3x - \mathbf{2y})$

$3x \times -2y = -6xy$

INSIDE: The terms on the inside are $-2y$ and $3x$: $(3x - \mathbf{2y})(\mathbf{3x} - 2y)$

$-2y \times 3x = -6xy$

LAST: The last terms in each set are $-2y$ and $-2y$: $(3x - \mathbf{2y})(3x - \mathbf{2y})$

$-2y \times -2y = 4y^2$

All of these individual results are put together for your final answer to the question.

$9x^2 - 6xy - 6xy + 4y^2 =$

$9x^2 - 12xy^2 + 4y^2$

### *Dividing Polynomials Using Long Division:*

You may also need to perform long division on polynomials on the exam.

A+

You can think of long division of the polynomial as reversing the FOIL operation. In other words, your result will generally be in one of the following formats: $(x + y)$ or $(x - y)$

Problem:

$(x^2 - x - 6) \div (x - 3) = ?$

A. $2x$

B. $x - 2$

C. $x - 2$

D. $y + 2$

E. $x + 2$

The correct answer is E.

In order to solve this type of problem, you must do long division of the polynomial.

Remember that you are subtracting the terms when you perform each part of the long division, so you need to be careful with negatives.

$$
\begin{array}{r}
x + 2 \\
x - 3 \overline{) x^2 - x - 6} \\
\underline{x^2 - 3x} \\
2x - 6 \\
\underline{2x - 6} \\
0
\end{array}
$$

### *Substituting Values in Polynomial Expressions:*

You may be asked to calculate the value of an expression by substituting its values. To solve these problems, put in the values for $x$ and $y$ and multiply. Then do the addition and subtraction.

Problem:

What is the value of the expression $4x^2 + 2xy - y^2$ when $x = 2$ and $y = -2$ ?

A. 4

B. 6

C. 8

D. 12

E. 14

The correct answer is A.

$4x^2 + 2xy - y^2 =$

$(4 \times 2^2) + (2 \times 2 \times -2) - (-2^2) =$

$(4 \times 2 \times 2) + (2 \times 2 \times -2) - (-2 \times -2) =$

$(4 \times 4) + (2 \times -4) - (4) =$

$16 + (-8) - 4 =$

$16 - 12 = 4$

## Operations on Polynomials Containing Three Terms:

You might also see problems on the exam in which you have to carry out operations on polynomial expressions that have more than two terms.

A+ | If you see polynomial expressions that have more than two terms inside each set of parentheses, remember to use the distributive property of multiplication to solve the problem.

To solve these types of problems, you will also need to understand basic exponent laws.

We will look at exponents in more detail in the "Law of Exponents" section.

Problem:

Perform the operation: $(5ab - 6a)(3ab^3 - 4b^2 - 3a)$

A. $15a^2b^4 - 20ab^3 - 15a^2b - 18a^2b^3 - 24ab^2 - 18a^2$

B. $15a^2b^4 - 20ab^3 - 15a^2b - 18a^2b^3 + 24ab^2 + 18a^2$

C. $15a^2b^4 - 20ab^3 - 15a^2b - 18a^2b^3 - 24ab^2 + 18a^2$

D. $15ab^4 - 20ab^3 - 15a^2b - 18a^2b^3 + 24ab^2 + 18a^2$

E. $-15a^2b^4 - 20ab^3 - 15a^2b - 18a^2b^3 + 24ab^2 + 18a^2$

The correct answer is B.

STEP 1: Apply the distributive property of multiplication by multiplying the first term in the first set of parentheses by all of the terms inside the second pair of parentheses.

Then multiply the second term from the first set of parentheses by all of the terms inside the second set of parentheses.

$(5ab - 6a)(3ab^3 - 4b^2 - 3a) =$

$(5ab \times 3ab^3) + (5ab \times -4b^2) + (5ab \times -3a) + (-6a \times 3ab^3) + (-6a \times -4b^2) + (-6a \times -3a)$

STEP 2: Add up the individual products in order to solve the problem.

$(5ab \times 3ab^3) + (5ab \times -4b^2) + (5ab \times -3a) + (-6a \times 3ab^3) + (-6a \times -4b^2) + (-6a \times -3a) =$

$$15a^2b^4 - 20ab^3 - 15a^2b - 18a^2b^3 + 24ab^2 + 18a^2$$

## Factoring Polynomials

Factoring means that you have to break down a polynomial into smaller parts.

You can factor by looking for integers or variables that are common to all of the terms of the equation.

In order to factor an equation, you must figure out what variables are common to each term of the equation.

### *Basic Factoring:*

Some problems will involve placing a term in front of a set of parentheses, as in the following example.

Problem:

Factor the following: $2xy - 6x^2y + 4x^2y^2$

A. $2xy(1 + 3x - 2xy)$

B. $2xy(1 - 3x + 2xy)$

C. $2xy(1 + 3x + 2xy)$

D. $2xy(1 - 3x - 2xy)$

E. $3xy(1 - 2x + 2xy)$

The correct answer is B.

Looking at this equation, we can see that each term contains $x$. We can also see that each term contains $y$.

So, first factor out $xy$.

$2xy - 6x^2y + 4x^2y^2 =$

$xy(2 - 6x + 4xy)$

Then, think about integers. We can see that all of the terms inside the parentheses are divisible by 2.

Now let's factor out the 2. To do this, we divide each term inside the parentheses by 2.

$xy(2 - 6x + 4xy) =$

$2xy(1 - 3x + 2xy)$

## *Factoring – Advanced Problems:*

You will also see problems like the one below that include more than one polynomial.

These types of problems often involve multiplying or dividing fractions that contain rational expressions.

In order to factor problems containing more than one polynomial, you will need to find the factors of the terms inside each set of parentheses.

We will look at this concept again in the section entitled "Fractions Containing Rational Expressions."

Problem:

Factor the following. Then simplify. $\dfrac{x^2 + 5x + 6}{x^2 + 6x + 8} \times \dfrac{x^2 + 4x}{x^2 + 8x + 15}$

A. $\dfrac{5}{x+5}$

B. $\dfrac{x}{x+5}$

C. $\dfrac{x+3}{x+4}$

D. $\dfrac{x+4}{x+3}$

E. $\dfrac{x^2}{x^2 + 8x}$

The correct answer is B.

$$\frac{x^2 + 5x + 6}{x^2 + 6x + 8} \times \frac{x^2 + 4x}{x^2 + 8x + 15} = ?$$

For this type of problem, first you need to find the factors of the numerators and denominators of each fraction.

When there are only addition signs in the rational expression, the factors will be in the following format:

( + )( + )

If there is a negative sign, then the factors will be in this format:

( + )( − )

You have to find the factors of the terms containing $x$ or $y$ variables, as well as the factors of the integers or other constants.

It is usually best to start with finding the factors of the final integer in each polynomial expression.

STEP 1: The numerator of the first fraction is $x^2 + 5x + 6$, so the final integer is 6.

The factors of 6 are:

1 × 6 = 6

2 × 3 = 6

Add these factors together to discover what integer you need to use in front of the second term of the expression.

1 + 6 = 7

2 + 3 = 5

2 and 3 satisfy both parts of the equation.

Therefore, the factors of $x^2 + 5x + 6$ are $(x + 2)(x + 3)$.

Now factor the other parts of the problem.

STEP 2: The denominator of the first fraction is $x^2 + 6x + 8$, so the final integer is 8.

The factors of 8 are:

1 × 8 = 8

2 × 4 = 8

Then add these factors together to find the integer to use in front of the second term of the expression.

1 + 8 = 9

2 + 4 = 6

Therefore, the factors of $x^2 + 6x + 8$ are $(x+2)(x+4)$.

STEP 3: The numerator of the second fraction is $x^2 + 4x$, so there is no final integer.

Because $x$ is common to both terms of the expression, the factor will be in this format:

$x(x + \quad )$

Therefore, in order to factor $x^2 + 4x$, we express it as $x(x+4)$.

STEP 4: The denominator of the second fraction is $x^2 + 8x + 15$, so the final integer is 15.

The factors of 15 are:

1 × 15 = 15

3 × 5 = 15

Add these factors together to find the integer to use in front of the second term of the expression.

1 + 15 = 16

3 + 5 = 8

Therefore, the factors of $x^2 + 8x + 15$ are $(x+3)(x+5)$.

A good shortcut for this type of problem is to remind yourself that it is a problem about factoring, so the factors you find in step 1 will probably be common to other parts of the expression.

In other words, we discovered in step 1 that the factors of $x^2 + 5x + 6$ are $(x+2)$ and $(x+3)$.

So, when you are factoring out the other parts of the problem, start with $(x+2)$ and $(x+3)$.

Now that we have completed all of the four steps above, we can set out our problem with the factors we discovered in each step.

We can see the factors of each fraction more clearly as follows:

$$\frac{x^2+5x+16}{x^2+6x+18}=\frac{(x+2)(x+3)}{(x+2)(x+4)} \qquad\qquad \frac{x^2+4x}{x^2+8x+15}=\frac{x(x+4)}{(x+3)(x+5)}$$

The problem should be set up as follows after you have found the factors:

$$\frac{x^2+5x+6}{x^2+6x+8}\times\frac{x^2+4x}{x^2+8x+15}=$$

$$\frac{(x+2)(x+3)}{(x+2)(x+4)}\times\frac{x(x+4)}{(x+3)(x+5)}$$

Then you need to simplify by removing the common factors.

Remove $(x+2)$ from the first fraction.

$$\frac{(x+2)(x+3)}{(x+2)(x+4)}\times\frac{x(x+4)}{(x+3)(x+5)}=$$

$$\frac{(x+3)}{(x+4)}\times\frac{x(x+4)}{(x+3)(x+5)}$$

Once you have simplified each fraction as much as possible, perform the operation indicated.

In this problem, we are multiplying. So, we can express the two factored-out fractions as one fraction and then remove the other common terms.

$$\frac{(x+3)}{(x+4)}\times\frac{x(x+4)}{(x+3)(x+5)}=$$

$$\frac{(x+3)(x+4)x}{(x+4)(x+3)(x+5)}$$

You can remove $(x+3)$ from the above fraction since it is in both the numerator and denominator.

$$\frac{(x+3)(x+4)x}{(x+4)(x+3)(x+5)} =$$

$$\frac{(x+4)x}{(x+4)(x+5)}$$

We can further simplify by removing $(x+4)$.

$$\frac{(x+4)x}{(x+4)(x+5)} =$$

$$\frac{x}{(x+5)}$$

So, our final answer is $\dfrac{x}{x+5}$

**Factoring to Find Possible Values of a Variable:**

You may see problems on the exam that give you a polynomial expression and ask you to determine possible values for the variables in the expression.

A+   | If you are asked to find values for variables such as $x$ or $y$ in a math problem, substitute zero for one variable. Then substitute zero for the other variable in order to solve the problem.

Problem:

What are two possible values of $x$ for the following equation? $x^2 + 6x + 8 = 0$

A.  1 and 2

B.  2 and 4

C.  6 and 8

D. −2 and −4

E. −3 and −4

The correct answer is D.

STEP 1: Factor the equation.

$x^2 + 6x + 8 = 0$

$(x + 2)(x + 4) = 0$

STEP 2: Now substitute 0 for $x$ in the first pair of parentheses.

$(0 + 2)(x + 4) = 0$

$2(x + 4) = 0$

$2x + 8 = 0$

$2x + 8 - 8 = 0 - 8$

$2x = -8$

$2x \div 2 = -8 \div 2$

$x = -4$

STEP 3: Then substitute 0 for $x$ in the second pair of parentheses.

$(x + 2)(x + 4) = 0$

$(x + 2)(0 + 4) = 0$

$(x + 2)4 = 0$

$4x + 8 = 0$

$4x + 8 - 8 = 0 - 8$

$4x = -8$

$4x \div 4 = -8 \div 4$

$x = -2$

**Fractions Containing Fractions**

On the college algebra part of the exam, you will see fractions that have fractions in their numerators or denominators.

A+   When you see fractions containing fractions, remember to treat the denominator as the division sign. Then invert the second fraction and multiply.

Problem:

$$\frac{x + \dfrac{1}{5}}{\dfrac{1}{x}} = \ ?$$

A. $x^2 + 5$

B. $\dfrac{x^3}{5}$

C. $x^2 + \dfrac{x}{5}$

D. $\dfrac{x + \dfrac{1}{5}}{x}$

E. $\dfrac{x}{x + \dfrac{1}{5}}$

The correct answer is C.

As stated above, the fraction can also be expressed as division.

$$\frac{x + \dfrac{1}{5}}{\dfrac{1}{x}} = \left(x + \frac{1}{5}\right) \div \frac{1}{x}$$

Then invert the second fraction and multiply the fractions as usual.

In this case $\dfrac{1}{x}$ becomes $\dfrac{x}{1}$ when inverted, which is then simplified to $x$.

$$\left(x + \frac{1}{5}\right) \div \frac{1}{x} =$$

$$\left(x + \frac{1}{5}\right) \times x =$$

$$x^2 + \frac{x}{5}$$

## Fractions Containing Radicals

You may see fractions that contain radicals in the numerator or denominator.

 **A+**

> If your problem has a fraction that contains a radical in its numerator or denominator, you need to eliminate the radical by multiplying both sides of the equation by the radical.

Problem:

If $\dfrac{30}{\sqrt{x^2 - 75}} = 6$, then $x$ = ?

A. 100

B. 30

C. 25

D. 10

E. 5

The correct answer is D.

Eliminate the radical in the denominator by multiplying both sides of the equation by the radical.

$$\frac{30}{\sqrt{x^2 - 75}} = 6$$

$$\frac{30}{\sqrt{x^2 - 75}} \times \sqrt{x^2 - 75} = 6 \times \sqrt{x^2 - 75}$$

$$30 = 6\sqrt{x^2 - 75}$$

Then eliminate the integer in front of the radical.

$$30 = 6\sqrt{x^2 - 75}$$

$$30 \div 6 = \left(6\sqrt{x^2 - 75}\right) \div 6$$

$$5 = \sqrt{x^2 - 75}$$

Then eliminate the radical by squaring both sides of the equation, and solve for $x$.

$$5 = \sqrt{x^2 - 75}$$

$$5^2 = \left(\sqrt{x^2 - 75}\right)^2$$

$$25 = x^2 - 75$$

$$25 + 75 = x^2 - 75 + 75$$

$$100 = x^2$$

$$x = 10$$

## Fractions Containing Rational Expressions

On the algebra and college-level math parts of the exam, you may see fractions that contain rational expressions.

Rational expressions are math problems that contain algebraic terms.

### *Adding and Subtracting Fractions Containing Rational Expressions:*

You may have to add or subtract two fractions that contain rational expressions.

 **A+** | To add or subtract two fractions that contain rational expressions, you need to calculate the lowest common denominator, just like you would for any other problem with fractions.

Problem :

$$\frac{x^5}{x^2 - 6x} + \frac{5}{x} = ?$$

A. $\dfrac{4 + x^6}{x^2 - 3x}$

B. $\dfrac{4x^2 - 16x}{x^7}$

C. $\dfrac{x^5 + 5x + 30}{x^2 - 6x}$

D. $\dfrac{x^5 + 5x - 30}{x^2 + 6x}$

E. $\dfrac{x^5 + 5x - 30}{x^2 - 6x}$

The correct answer is E.

Find the lowest common denominator. Since $x$ is common to both denominators, we can convert the denominator of the second fraction to the LCD by multiplying by $(x - 6)$.

$$\frac{x^5}{x^2 - 6x} + \frac{5}{x} =$$

$$\frac{x^5}{x^2 - 6x} + \left(\frac{5}{x} \times \frac{x - 6}{x - 6}\right) =$$

$$\frac{x^5}{x^2 - 6x} + \frac{5x - 30}{x^2 - 6x} =$$

$$\frac{x^5 + 5x - 30}{x^2 - 6x}$$

**Multiplying Fractions Containing Rational Expressions:**

The following problem asks you to multiply two fractions, both of which contain rational expressions.

 To multiply fractions containing rational expressions, multiply the numerator of the first fraction by the numerator of the second fraction to get the new numerator. Then multiply the denominators.

Problem:

$$\frac{2x^3}{5} \times \frac{4}{x^2} = ?$$

A. $\dfrac{8x}{5}$

B. $\dfrac{5}{8x}$

C. $\dfrac{8}{5}$

D. $8x$

E. $5x$

The correct answer is A.

Multiply the numerator of the first fraction by the numerator of the second fraction. Then multiply the denominators.

$$\frac{2x^3}{5} \times \frac{4}{x^2} = \frac{8x^3}{5x^2}$$

Then factor the numerator and denominator.

As stated previously, we will discuss operations on exponents in more depth in the "Laws of Exponents" section of the study guide.

$$\frac{8x^3}{5x^2} = \frac{8x(x^2)}{5(x^2)}$$

Then we can cancel out $x^2$ to solve the problem.

$$\frac{8x(x^2)}{5(x^2)} = \frac{8x}{5}$$

## *Dividing Fractions Containing Rational Expressions:*

You may also be asked to divide two fractions, both of which contain rational expressions.

 In order to divide fractions that contain rational expressions, invert the second fraction and multiply. Then cancel out any common factors. Be sure to cancel out completely.

Problem:

$$\frac{6x+6}{x^2} \div \frac{3x+3}{x^3} = ?$$

A. $2x$

B. $6x$

C. $18x^3$

D. $\dfrac{3x+3}{x}$

E. $\dfrac{18x^2+18}{x^5}$

The correct answer is A.

The first step in solving the problem is to invert and multiply by the second fraction.

$$\frac{6x+6}{x^2} \div \frac{3x+3}{x^3} =$$

$$\frac{6x+6}{x^2} \times \frac{x^3}{3x+3} =$$

$$\frac{x^3(6x+6)}{x^2(3x+3)}$$

Then factor the numerator and denominator. $(x + 1)$ is common to both the numerator and the denominator, so we can factor that out.

$$\frac{x^3(6x+6)}{x^2(3x+3)} =$$

$$\frac{x^3 6(x+1)}{x^2 3(x+1)}$$

Now cancel out the $(x + 1)$.

$$\frac{x^3 6(x+1)}{x^2 3(x+1)} =$$

$$\frac{x^3 6}{x^2 3} =$$

$$\frac{6x^3}{3x^2}$$

Now factor out $x^2$ and cancel it out.

$$\frac{6x^3}{3x^2} =$$

$$\frac{6x \times x^2}{3x^2} =$$

$$\frac{6x}{3}$$

The numerator and denominator share the factor of 3, so cancel out further in order to get your final result.

$$\frac{6x}{3} =$$

$$\frac{3 \times 2 \times x}{3} =$$

$$2x$$

## Imaginary and Complex Numbers

Imaginary numbers are not real numbers. That is to say, imaginary numbers are not whole numbers, integers, decimals, or fractions.

You will need to know some basic laws of imaginary numbers for the exam, as well as how to perform some basic operations with imaginary numbers.

 Two complex numbers are equal if and only if their real parts are equal and their imaginary parts are equal.

Complex numbers contain a real component and an imaginary component.

Problem:

$x$ and $y$ are real numbers. $ai$ and $bi$ are complex numbers.

When does $ai + x = bi + y$ ?

A. When $a = b$

B. When $x = y$

C. When $ai = bi$ and $x = y$

D. When $ai = y$ and $bi = x$

E. When $a = x$ and $b = y$

The correct answer is C.

As mentioned above, two complex numbers are equal if and only if their real parts are equal and their imaginary parts are equal.

For $ai + x$ to be equal to $bi + y$, $ai$ must be equal to $bi$ and $x$ must be equal to $y$.

## Inequalities

Inequality problems will have a less than or greater than sign.

There may be more than one equation in a single inequality problem on the Accuplacer exam.

When solving inequality problems, isolate integers before dealing with any fractions. Also remember that if you multiply an inequality by a negative number, you have to reverse the direction of the less than or greater than sign.

Problem 1:

$40 - \dfrac{3x}{5} \geq 10$, then $x \leq$ ?

A. 15

B. 30

C. 40

D. 50

E. 75

The correct answer is D.

Deal with the whole numbers on each side of the equation first.

$$40 - \frac{3x}{5} \geq 10$$

$$(40 - 40) - \frac{3x}{5} \geq 10 - 40$$

$$-\frac{3x}{5} \geq -30$$

Then deal with the fraction.

$$-\frac{3x}{5} \geq -30$$

$$\left(5 \times -\frac{3x}{5}\right) \geq -30 \times 5$$

$$-3x \geq -30 \times 5$$

$$-3x \geq -150$$

Then deal with the remaining whole numbers.

$-3x \geq -150$

$-3x \div 3 \geq -150 \div 3$

$-x \geq -150 \div 3$

$-x \geq -50$

Then deal with the negative number.

$-x \geq -50$

$-x + 50 \geq -50 + 50$

$-x + 50 \geq 0$

Finally, isolate the unknown variable as a positive number.

$-x + 50 \geq 0$

$-x + x + 50 \geq 0 + x$

$50 \geq x$

$x \leq 50$

Problem 2:

Inequalities may also be expressed in practical problems like the one below.

In the equations below, $x$ represents the cost of one online game and $y$ represents the cost of one movie ticket.

If $x - 2 > 5$ and $y = x - 2$, then the cost of 2 discounted movie tickets is greater than which one of the following?

A. $x - 2$

B. $x - 5$

C. $y + 5$

D. 5

E. 10

The correct answer is E.

For problems like this, look to see if both of the equations have any variables or terms in common.

In this problem, both equations contain $x - 2$.

The cost of one movie ticket is represented by $y$, and $y$ is equal to $x - 2$.

Therefore, we can substitute values from one equation to another.

$x - 2 > 5$

$y > 5$

If two tickets are being purchased, we need to solve for $2y$.

$y \times 2 > 5 \times 2$

$2y > 10$

## Laws of Exponents

You will need to know exponent laws very well for the examination.

You will see questions that involve adding and subtracting exponents, exponents containing fractions, and exponents that contain negative numbers.

You may also see practical problems that contain exponents.

A+    When the base numbers are the same and you need to multiply, you add the exponents. When the base numbers are the same and you need to divide, you subtract the exponents.

We can prove the above concepts as shown below.

For multiplication:

$2^3 \times 2^2 = 2^5$

$8 \times 4 = 32$

$2^5 = 2 \times 2 \times 2 \times 2 \times 2 = 32$

For division:

$$2^3 \div 2^2 = 2^1 = 2$$

$$8 \div 4 = 2$$

Now try the problems that follow.

## Adding and subtracting exponents:

Problem 1:

$$11^5 \times 11^3 = ?$$

A. $11^8$

B. $11^{15}$

C. $22^8$

D. $121^8$

E. $121^{15}$

The correct answer is A.

The base number in this example is 11.

So, we add the exponents: $5 + 3 = 8$

That is:

$$11^5 \times 11^3 =$$

$$11^{(5 + 3)} =$$

$$11^8$$

Problem 2:

$$10^6 \div 10^4 = ?$$

A. $10^{24}$

B. $10^2$

C. $20^{24}$

D. $20^2$

E. $100^2$

The correct answer is B.

The base number in this example is 10.

So, we subtract the exponents: $6 - 4 = 2$

$10^6 \div 10^4 =$

$10^{(6 - 4)} =$

$10^2$

Problem 3:

Now try this practical problem, using the laws of exponents stated above.

A flight with a low-cost airline travels $9 \times 10^2$ miles per hour for $3 \times 10^{-1}$ hours.

How far has this flight traveled?

A.   135 miles

B.   270 miles

C.   900 miles

D. 1350 miles

E. 2700 miles

The correct answer is B.

We need to multiply, so you add the exponents.

In this problem, we have to multiply the miles per hour times the number of hours in order to calculate the distance traveled.

Since we have the base number of 10 for each number that has an exponent, we can add the exponent of 2 to the exponent of −1.

($9 \times 10^2$ miles per hour) × ($3 \times 10^{-1}$ hours) =

$9 \times 3 \times 10^{(2 + -1)} =$

$9 \times 3 \times 10^1 =$

$9 \times 3 \times 10 = 270$ miles

**Fractions as exponents:**

You will see problems that have exponents in their fractions, like the examples that follow.

Example 1: $x^{1/2} = (\sqrt[2]{x})^1 = \sqrt{x}$

Example 2: $x^{3/7} = (\sqrt[7]{x})^3$

Place the base number inside the radical sign. The denominator of the exponent is the $n^{th}$ root of the radical. The numerator is new exponent.

Problem:

$x^{4/9} = ?$

A. $\dfrac{4x}{9}$

B. $(\sqrt[9]{x})^4$

C. $(\sqrt[9]{x})^5$

D. $(\sqrt[5]{x})^9$

E. $(\sqrt[4]{x})^9$

The correct answer is B.

Place the base number inside the radical sign. The denominator of the exponent is the $n^{th}$ root of the radical. The numerator is new exponent.

$x^{4/9} =$

$(\sqrt[9]{x})^4$

## Negative exponents:

You will see rational expressions that contain negative numbers in their exponents.

For example: $x^{-2} = \dfrac{1}{x^2}$

Remove the negative sign on the exponent by expressing the number as a fraction, with 1 as the numerator. Then place the number with the exponent in the denominator.

Problem:

$x^{-6} = ?$

A. $\dfrac{1}{x^{-6}}$

B. $\dfrac{1}{x^6}$

C. $-6x$

D. $\dfrac{1}{-6x}$

E. $\dfrac{-1}{x^6}$

The correct answer is B.

Remove the negative sign on the exponent. Set up a fraction, with 1 as the numerator. Place the number with the exponent in the denominator.

$$x^{-6} = \dfrac{1}{x^6}$$

## Zero exponent:

You may see rational expressions that have 0 as an exponent.

Any number, apart from zero, is equal to 1 when raised to the power of zero. Example: $x^0 = 1$

Problem:

$3^0 = ?$

A. –3

B. 0

C. 1

D. 3

E. $\frac{1}{3}$

The correct answer is C.

Any non-zero number raised to the power of zero is equal to 1.

**Logarithmic functions**

Logarithmic functions are just another way of expressing exponents.

$x = \log_y Z$ is always the same as: $y^x = Z$
Be sure to check your result by performing the exponential operation.

Problem:

$2 = \log_5 25$ is equivalent to which of the following?

A. $2^5$

B. $5^2$

C. $10^2$

D. $25^2$

E. $50^2$

The correct answer is B.

Solve by substituting values into the equation.

$x = \log_y Z$ is always the same as $y^x = Z$

$2 = \log_5 25$ is the same as $5^2 = 25$

Then check your answer by performing the operation on the number with the exponent.

$5^2 = 25$

$5 \times 5 = 25$

## Matrices

Matrices are represented in a box-like format, consisting of 4 numbers.

Two numbers will be at the top of the matrix, and two numbers will be directly below these on the bottom of the matrix.

You will need to know how to add and subtract matrices for the exam.

In order to add two matrices, you need to add the numbers from each matrix to the numbers of the other matrix that are located in the same positions. Then place these results in a new matrix.

Problem:

Consider the following matrices.

Matrix A

$$\begin{bmatrix} -1 & 4 \\ -7 & 8 \end{bmatrix}$$

Matrix B

$$\begin{bmatrix} -3 & 2 \\ 3 & -2 \end{bmatrix}$$

What is A + B?

A. $\begin{bmatrix} 2 & 2 \\ -10 & 10 \end{bmatrix}$

B. $\begin{bmatrix} 2 & -2 \\ 10 & -10 \end{bmatrix}$

C. $\begin{bmatrix} -4 & 6 \\ -4 & 6 \end{bmatrix}$

D. $\begin{bmatrix} 4 & -6 \\ 4 & -6 \end{bmatrix}$

E. $\begin{bmatrix} 4 & 6 \\ 4 & 6 \end{bmatrix}$

The correct answer is C.

Add the numbers from each matrix in each position to the numbers of the other matrix that are located in the corresponding positions.

Upper left: −1 + −3 = −4

Upper right: 4 + 2 = 6

Lower left: −7 + 3 = −4

Lower right: 8 + −2 = 6

These numbers form the new matrix as shown below.

$\begin{bmatrix} -4 & 6 \\ -4 & 6 \end{bmatrix}$

### *Determinants:*

If you are asked to find the determinant of a matrix, you need to cross multiply and subtract.

So, for example:

$\begin{bmatrix} 2 & 3 \\ 5 & 4 \end{bmatrix}$

The determinant is (2 × 4) − (5 × 3) = 8 − 15 = −7

### Multiple Solutions

You will see questions on the exam that give you an equation and then ask you how many solutions there are for the equation provided.

 You will need to consider both positive and negative numbers as potential solutions.

Problem 1:

How many solutions exist for the following equation?

$x^2 + 8 = 0$

A. 0

B. 1

C. 2

D. 4

E. 8

The correct answer is A.

Remember that any real number squared will always equal a positive number.

Since 8 is added to the first value $x^2$, the result will always be 8 or greater.

In other words, since $x^2$ is always a positive number, the result of the equation would never be 0.

So, there are zero solutions for this equation.

Problem 2:

How many solutions exist for the following equation?

$x^2 - 9 = 0$

A. 0

B. 1

C. 2

D. 4

E. 8

The correct answer is C.

Any real number squared will always equal a positive number.

Since 9 is subtracted from $x^2$, $x^2$ needs to be equal to 9.

Both 3 and −3 solve the equation. So, there are two solutions for this equation.

**Scientific notation**

Scientific notation means that you have to state the given number as a multiple of $10^2$, in other words, as a factor of 100.

For example, in scientific notation, the number 517 is $5.17 \times 10^2$.

In order to express a number in scientific notation, divide the given number by 100. Then express your answer as a factor of that result and $10^2$.

Problem:

Express 784 in scientific notation.

A. $7840 \times \frac{1}{10}$

B. $784 \times \frac{10}{10}$

C. $78.4 \times 10$

D. $7.84 \times 10$

E. $7.84 \times 10^2$

The correct answer is E.

**Sequences and Series – Arithmetic Sequences and Series**

Sequences are numbers in a list like the following: 1, 3, 5, 7, 9

In a series, the numbers are added: $1 + 3 + 5 + 7 + 9$

In an arithmetic sequence, the difference between one number and the next is known as a constant.

In other words, you add the same value each time until you reach the end of the sequence.

The formula for the nth number of an arithmetic sequence is $a + [d \times (n - 1)]$, where variable $a$ represents the starting number and variable $d$ represents the difference or constant.

Problem:

What is the next number in the following sequence?

1, 5, 9, 13, 17, . . .

A. 20

B. 21

C. 30

D. 40

E. 45

The correct answer is B.

There is a difference of 4 between each number in the above sequence.

Where variable *a* represents your starting number and variable *d* represents the difference, you could write an arithmetic sequence like this:

a, a + d, a + 2d, a + 3d, a + 4d, a + 5d, . . .

However, it is easier to remember that the formula for the nth number of an arithmetic sequence is:

a + [d × (n-1)]

We can prove that 21 is the sixth number of the sequence in our problem by putting the values into the formula.

a = 1

d = 4

n = 6

a + [d × (n − 1)]

1 + [4 × (6 − 1)] =

1 + (4 × 5) =

1 + 20 = 21

## Sequences and Series – Geometric Sequences and Series

When the sequence cannot be solved by addition, then you usually have a geometric sequence.

In a geometric sequence, each number is found by multiplying the previous term by a factor known as a common ratio.

Where the first number is represented by variable $a$ and the factor (called the "common ratio") is represented by variable $r$, the formula for calculating the $n^{th}$ item in a geometric sequence is: $ar^{(n-1)}$

Problem:

What is the next number in the following sequence?

2, 6, 18, 54, . . .

A.  60

B.  72

C.  80

D. 162

E. 242

The correct answer is D.

Each number in the above sequence is found by multiplying by a factor of 3.

$2 \times 3 = 6$

$6 \times 3 = 18$

$18 \times 3 = 54$

So, each subsequent number is found by multiplying the previous number by 3.

Where the first number is represented by variable $a$ and the factor (called the "common ratio") is represented by variable $r$, you could write out a geometric sequence like this:

$a, ar, a(r)^2, a(r)^3$ . . .

The sequence in this problem starts at 2 and triples each time, so a = 2 (the first term) and r = 3 (the "common ratio").

Remember that the formula for calculating the n$^{th}$ item in a geometric sequence is as follows:

$ar^{(n-1)}$

So, let's consider our example problem again.

2, 6, 18, 54, . . .

The fifth term of the sequence is 54 × 3 = 162.

We can check this by putting the values into our formula.

a = 2 (the first term)

r = 3 (the "common ratio")

n = 5

$ar^{(n-1)}$

$2 \times 3^{(5-1)} =$

$2 \times 3^4 =$

2 × 81 = 162

**Sigma Notation**

The symbol $\sum$ is known as the sigma notation.

When you see the sigma notation, you have to perform the operation at the right-hand side of the sigma sign.

Perform the operation at the right-hand side of the sigma sign by substituting the value provided at the bottom of the sigma sign.

Repeat the operation for every subsequent value, up to and including the value at the top of the sigma sign.

Then sum up the individual results for each operation to get the answer.

For problems with the sigma notation, repeat the given operation for every value, from the value stated at the bottom of the sigma sign the value at the top of the sigma sign.

Problem:

Find the value of the following:

$$\sum_{x=2}^{5} x + 2$$

A. 6

B. 7

C. 8

D. 12

E. 22

The correct answer is E.

You need to perform the operation at the right-hand side of the sigma sign.

In this problem, we perform the operation for $x = 2$, $x = 3$, $x = 4$, and $x = 5$ (because 5 is the number at the top).

For $x = 2$:  $x + 2 = 2 + 2 = 4$

For $x = 3$:  $x + 2 = 3 + 2 = 5$

For $x = 4$:  $x + 2 = 4 + 2 = 6$

For $x = 5$:  $x + 2 = 5 + 2 = 7$

Then we add these individual sums together to get the final result.

$4 + 5 + 6 + 7 = 22$

**Solving by Elimination**

When you have to solve a problem by elimination, you will see two equations as in the following question.

 A+ | In order to solve by elimination, you need to subtract the second equation from the first equation.

Problem:

Solve the following by elimination.

$x + 4y = 30$

$2x + 2y = 36$

A. $x = 2$ and $y = 7$

B. $x = 4$ and $y = 14$

C. $x = 14$ and $y = 4$

D. $x = 16$ and $y = 2$

E. $x = 18$ and $y = 3$

The correct answer is C.

Look at the $x$ term of the second equation, which is $2x$.

In order to eliminate the $x$ variable, we need to multiply the first equation by $2$ and then subtract the second equation from this result.

$x + 4y = 30$

$(2 \times x) + (2 \times 4y) = (30 \times 2)$

$2x + 8y = 60$

Now subtract the two equations.

$2x + 8y = 60$

$$\frac{-(2x+2y=36)}{6y=24}$$

Then solve for $y$.

$6y = 24$

$6y \div 6 = 24 \div 6$

$y = 4$

Using our first equation $x + 4y = 30$, substitute the value of 4 for $y$ to solve for $x$.

$x + 4y = 30$

$x + (4 \times 4) = 30$

$x + 16 = 30$

$x + 16 - 16 = 30 - 16$

$x = 14$

## Solving for an Unknown Variable

You will certainly see problems involving solving equations for an unknown variable on the exam.

 Perform the multiplication on the items in parentheses first. Then eliminate the integers and solve for $x$.

Problem:

If $3x - 2(x + 5) = -8$, then $x = ?$

A. 1

B. 2

C. 3

D. 5

E. 6

The correct answer is B.

To solve this type of problem, do multiplication on the items in parentheses first.

$3x - 2(x + 5) = -8$

$3x - 2x - 10 = -8$

Then deal with the integers by putting them on one side of the equation.

$3x - 2x - 10 + 10 = -8 + 10$

$3x - 2x = 2$

Then solve for $x$.

$3x - 2x = 2$

$1x = 2$

$x = 2$

## Special Operations

Equations with special operations will show a character which is not a mathematical symbol, such as # or Б.

Look at the relationship between the left-hand side and the right-hand side of the equation to determine which operations you need to perform on any new equation containing the special operation.

Problem:

If Д is a special operation defined by $(x \text{ Д } y) = (5x \div 4y)$ and $(8 \text{ Д } y) = 5$, then $y = ?$

A.   16

B.   4

C.   2

D.  0.25

E.  0.50

The correct answer is C.

We have the special operation defined as $(x Д y) = (5x ÷ 4y)$.

Looking at the relationship between the left-hand side and the right-hand side of this equation, we can determine the operations that need to be performed on any new equation containing the operation Д and variables $x$ and $y$.

For our problem, the new equation will be carried out as follows:

Operation Д is division.

The number or variable immediately after the opening parenthesis is multiplied by 5.

The number or variable immediately before the closing parenthesis is multiplied by 4.

So, the new equation $(8 Д y) = 5$ becomes $(5 × 8) ÷ (4 × y) = 5$

Now solve for $y$:

$(5 × 8) ÷ (4 × y) = 5$

$40 ÷ 4y = 5$

$40 ÷ 4y × 4y = 5 × 4y$

$40 = 5 × 4y$

$40 = 20y$

$40 ÷ 20 = 20y ÷ 20$

$y = 2$

**Square Roots, Cube Roots, and Other Radicals**

Square roots and cube roots are sometimes referred to as radicals.

You will need to know how to perform the operations of multiplication and division on square and cube roots.

You will also see problems that involve rationalizing and factoring square and cube roots.

*Factoring radicals:*

Factoring radicals requires the same concepts as factoring integers or polynomial expressions.

You have to find the factors of the numbers inside the square root symbols.

In order to factor a radical, you need to find the squared factors of the number inside the radical sign. For example:

$$\sqrt{128} = \sqrt{64 \times 2} = \sqrt{8 \times 8 \times 2} = 8\sqrt{2}$$

Problem 1:

Which of the answers below is equal to the following radical expression? $\sqrt{45}$

A. $1 \div 45$

B. $5\sqrt{9}$

C. $9\sqrt{5}$

D. $3\sqrt{5}$

E. $5\sqrt{3}$

The correct answer is D.

For square root problems like this one, you need to remember certain mathematical principles.

First, remember to factor the number inside the square root sign.

The factors of 45 are:

$1 \times 45 = 45$

$3 \times 15 = 45$

$5 \times 9 = 45$

Then look to see if any of these factors have square roots that are whole numbers.

In this case, the only factor whose square root is a whole number is 9.

Now find the square root of 9.

$\sqrt{9} = 3$

Finally, you need to put this number at the front of the square root sign and put the other factor inside the square root sign in order to solve the problem.

$$\sqrt{45} =$$

$$\sqrt{9 \times 5} =$$

$$\sqrt{3 \times 3 \times 5} =$$

$$3\sqrt{5}$$

Problem 2:

Your may see advanced problems on radicals involving other operations, such as addition or subtraction.

$$\sqrt{32} + 2\sqrt{72} + 3\sqrt{18} = ?$$

A. $2\sqrt{16} + 2\sqrt{36} + 3\sqrt{9}$

B. $5\sqrt{122}$

C. $6\sqrt{122}$

D. $21\sqrt{2}$

E. $25\sqrt{2}$

The correct answer is E.

First you need to find the squared factors of the amounts inside the radical signs.

In this problem, 16, 36, and 9 are squared factors of each radical because $16 = 4^2$, $36 = 6^2$, and $9 = 3^2$.

$$\sqrt{32} + 2\sqrt{72} + 3\sqrt{18} =$$

$$\sqrt{2 \times 16} + 2\sqrt{2 \times 36} + 3\sqrt{2 \times 9}$$

Then expand the amounts inside the radicals for the factors and simplify.

$$\sqrt{2\times16}+2\sqrt{2\times36}+3\sqrt{2\times9}=$$

$$\sqrt{2\times(4\times4)}+2\sqrt{2\times(6\times6)}+3\sqrt{2\times(3\times3)}=$$

$$4\sqrt{2}+(2\times6)\sqrt{2}+(3\times3)\sqrt{2}=$$

$$4\sqrt{2}+12\sqrt{2}+9\sqrt{2}=$$

$$25\sqrt{2}$$

**Multiplication of radicals:**

To multiply radicals, multiply the numbers inside the square root signs. Then put this result inside a square root symbol for your answer. For example: $\sqrt{x}\times\sqrt{y}=\sqrt{xy}$

Problem:

$\sqrt{6}\times\sqrt{5}=$ ?

A. $\sqrt{30}$

B. $\sqrt{11}$

C. $6\sqrt{5}$

D. $5\sqrt{6}$

E. $\sqrt{-1}$

The correct answer is A.

Multiply the numbers inside the square root signs first.

$6\times5=30$

Then put this result inside a square root symbol for your answer.

$\sqrt{30}$

### *Rationalizing radicals:*

You may see problems on the exam that ask you to rationalize a number or to express a radical number as a rational number.

 Perform the necessary mathematical operations in order to remove the square root symbol. This normally involves factoring in order to find square or cube roots.

Problem:

Express as a rational number: $\sqrt[3]{\dfrac{27}{64}}$

A. $\dfrac{1}{3}$

B. $\dfrac{4}{3}$

C. $\dfrac{3}{4}$

D. $\dfrac{64}{27}$

E. $\dfrac{27}{64}$

The correct answer is C.

In this problem, you have to find the cube roots of the numerator and denominator in order to eliminate the radical.

Remember that the cube root is the number which satisfies the equation when multiplied by itself two times.

$$\sqrt[3]{\dfrac{27}{64}} = \sqrt[3]{\dfrac{3 \times 3 \times 3}{4 \times 4 \times 4}} = \dfrac{3}{4}$$

## Systems of Equations

For these problems, you will see two equations, both of which will contain $x$ and $y$.

In one equation, $x$ and $y$ will be added. In the other equation, $x$ and $y$ will be multiplied.

In order to solve systems of equations, look at the equation that contains multiplication first. Then find the factors of the product in the equation to solve the problem.

Problem:

What ordered pair is a solution to the following system of equations?

$x + y = 9$

$xy = 20$

A. (2, 7)

B. (2,10)

C. (3, 6)

D. (5, 3)

E. (4, 5)

The correct answer is E.

For questions on systems of equations like this one, you should look at the multiplication equation first.

Ask yourself, what are the factors of 20?

We know that 20 is the product of the following:

$1 \times 20 = 20$

$2 \times 10 = 20$

$4 \times 5 = 20$

Now add each of the two factors together to solve the first equation.

$1 + 20 = 21$

2 + 10 = 12

4 + 5 = 9

(4, 5) solves both equations, so it is the correct answer.

**Geometry concepts and formulas:**

Geometry problems on the test will cover both coordinate geometry and plane geometry.

You will need to know coordinate geometry for problems like:

- Calculating the slope of the line

- Determining the midpoint between two points

- Finding $x$ and $y$ intercepts

- Using the distance formula to find the distance between two points on a line

Basic coordinate geometry is included in the algebra section of the Accuplacer Test because you need to understand how to use algebraic principles in order to solve certain coordinate geometry problems.

You will also need to know plane geometry for the college math part of the exam.

Plane geometry includes calculations relating to geometric figures such as:

- Triangles

- Squares

- Rectangles

- Circles

- Arcs

- Cones, Cylinders, and Other 3-D Shapes

- Hybrid figures

**Angle Measurement**

For angle measurement questions, you need to remember these concepts:

The sum of all three angles in a triangle is always 180°.

Two sides of an isosceles triangle are equal in length, and their corresponding angles are also equal.

For an isosceles triangle, deduct the degrees given from 180° to find out the total degrees of the two other angles.

Problem:

Consider the isosceles triangle in the diagram below.

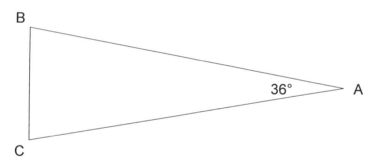

What is the measurement of ∠B?

A.  36°

B.  45°

C.  72°

D.  144°

E. Cannot be determined from the information provided.

The correct answer is C.

Remember that we need to deduct the degrees given from 180° to find out the total degrees of the two other angles.

180° − 36° = 144°

Now divide this result by two in order to find out how many degrees each angle has.

144° ÷ 2 = 72°

## Arcs

Arc length is the distance on the outside of a circle.

In other words, you can think of arc length as the partial circumference of a circle.

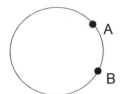

The distance between A and B above is arc AB.

 You can calculate the radius or diameter of a circle if you have the measurement of a central angle and the length of the arc subtending the central angle.

If you do not know how to calculate the circumference of a circle, please refer to the section on circumference before you attempt the problem below.

Problem:

The central angle in the circle below measures 60° and is subtended by an arc which is $7\pi$ centimeters in length. How many centimeters long is the radius of this circle?

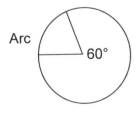

A. 42

B. 21

C. $6\pi$

D. 6

E. 7

The correct answer is B.

Circumference = $\pi \times$ radius $\times$ 2

The angle given in the problem is 60°.

If we divide the total 360° in the circle by the 60° angle, we have: 360 ÷ 60 = 6

So, there are 6 such arcs along this circle.

We then have to multiply the number of arcs by the length of each arc to get the circumference of the circle.

$6 \times 7\pi = 42\pi$  (circumference)

Then, use the formula for the circumference of the circle to solve.

Circumference = $\pi \times$ radius $\times$ 2

$42\pi = \pi \times 2 \times$ radius

$42\pi \div 2 = \pi \times 2 \times$ radius $\div 2$

$21\pi = \pi \times$ radius

$21 =$ radius

## Area

You will need to calculate the area of geometric shapes, such as circles, squares, triangles, and rectangles for the test.

Be sure that you know the following formulas from memory for the exam.

When you have memorized the formulas, attempt the problems that follow.

Area of a circle: $\pi \times r^2$ (radius squared)
Area of a square or rectangle: length × width
Area of a triangle: (base × height) ÷ 2

Problem 1:

A football field is 100 yards long and 30 yards wide. What is the area of the football field in square yards?

A. 130

B. 150

C. 300

D. 1500

E. 3000

The correct answer is E.

The area of a rectangle is equal to its length times its width.

This football field is 30 yards wide and 100 yards long, we now we can substitute the values.

rectangle area = width × length

rectangle area = 30 × 100

rectangle area = 3000

Problem 2:

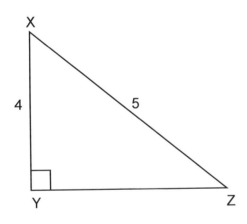

In the figure above, XY is 4 inches long and XZ is 5 inches long.

What is the area of triangle XYZ?

A. 3

B. 5

C. 6

D. 10

E. 12

The correct answer is C.

In order to calculate the area of a triangle, you need this formula:

triangle area = (base × height) ÷ 2

However, the base length of the triangle described in the problem, which is line segment YZ, is not given.

So, we need to calculate the base length using the Pythagorean theorem.

We will look at the Pythagorean theorem again in the "Hypotenuse Length" section of the study guide.

We will state briefly here that according to the Pythagorean theorem, the length of the hypotenuse is equal to the square root of the sum of the squares of the two other sides.

$$\sqrt{4^2 + base^2} = 5$$

$$\sqrt{16 + base^2} = 5$$

Now square each side of the equation in order to solve for the base length.

$$\sqrt{16 + base^2} = 5$$

$$(\sqrt{16 + base^2})^2 = 5^2$$

$$16 + base^2 = 25$$

$$16 - 16 + base^2 = 25 - 16$$

$$base^2 = 9$$

$$\sqrt{base^2} = \sqrt{9}$$

$$base = 3$$

Now solve for the area of the triangle.

triangle area = (base × height) ÷ 2

triangle area = (3 × 4) ÷ 2

triangle area = 12 ÷ 2

triangle area = 6

## Circumference

The circumference is the measurement around the outside of a circle.

You can think of circumference like perimeter, except circumference is used in calculations for round objects, rather than for shapes like squares or rectangles.

The formula for the circumference of a circle is: π × diameter
Remember that diameter = radius × 2

We will look at advanced problems on diameter in the "Diameter" section of the study guide.

Problem:

If a circle has a diameter of 12, what is the circumference of the circle?

A.   6π

B.  12π

C.  24π

D.  36π

E.  144π

The correct answer is B.

Substitute the value into the formula.

circumference = diameter × π

circumference = 12π

Remember not to confuse the formula for the circumference of a circle with the formula for the area of a circle.

circle area = radius$^2$ × π

**Diameter**

You will need to know how to use diameter to calculate the circumference or area of a circle for geometry problems on the exam.

You will also need to know how to calculate diameter itself using the facts stated in advanced math problems, like the problem that follows.

 Diameter is the measurement across the entire width of a circle. Diameter is always double the radius.

Problem:

If a circle with center (−6, 6) is tangent to the x axis in the standard (x, y) coordinate plane, what is the diameter of the circle?

A.  −6

B. −12

C.  6

D.  12

E.  36

The correct answer is D.

Remember that if the center of a circle (x, y) is tangent to the x axis, then both of the following conditions are true:

(1) The point of tangency is equal to (x, 0).

AND

(2) The distance between (x, y) and (x, 0) is equal to the radius.

The center of this circle is (−6, 6) and the point of tangency is (−6, 0).

So, we need to subtract these two coordinates in order to find the length of the radius.

(−6, 6) − (−6, 0) = (0, 6)

In other words, the radius length is 6, so the diameter length is 12.

**Distance formula**

The distance formula is used to calculate the linear distance between two points on a two-dimensional graph.

The two points are represented by the coordinates $(x_1, y_1)$ and $(x_2, y_2)$.

 **A+** | The distance formula is as follows: $d = \sqrt{(x_2 - x_1)^2 + (y_2 - y_1)^2}$

Problem:

What is the distance between (1,0) and (5,4)?

A. 4

B. 5

C. 16

D. $\sqrt{18}$

E. $\sqrt{32}$

The correct answer is E.

Substitute values into the distance formula from the facts stated in the problem.

$$d = \sqrt{(x_2 - x_1)^2 + (y_2 - y_1)^2}$$

$$d = \sqrt{(5 - 1)^2 + (4 - 0)^2}$$

$$d = \sqrt{4^2 + 4^2}$$

$$d = \sqrt{16 + 16}$$

$$d = \sqrt{32}$$

**Hypotenuse length**

The hypotenuse is the side of the triangle that is opposite to the right angle.

In other words, the hypotenuse is opposite to the square corner of the triangle.

To calculate the length of the hypotenuse in right triangles, you will need the Pythagorean theorem.

According to the theorem, the length of the hypotenuse (represented by side C) is equal to the square root of the sum of the squares of the other two sides of the triangle (represented by A and B).

A+

For any right triangle with sides A, B, and C, you need to remember this formula:

hypotenuse length $C = \sqrt{A^2 + B^2}$

Problem 1:

If one leg of a triangle is 5cm and the other leg is 12cm, what is the measurement of the hypotenuse of the triangle?

A. $5\sqrt{12}$ cm

B. $12\sqrt{5}$ cm

C. $\sqrt{17}$ cm

D. 13 cm

E. 17 cm

The correct answer is D.

Substitute the values into the formula in order to find the solution for this problem:

$\sqrt{A^2 + B^2}$ = C

$\sqrt{5^2 + 12^2}$ = C

$\sqrt{25 + 144}$ = C

$\sqrt{169} = C$

13 cm

Problem 2:

In the figure below, ∠Y is a right angle and ∠X = 60°.

If line segment YZ is 5 units long, then how long is line segment XY?

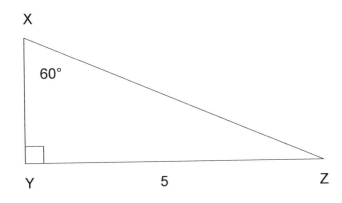

A. 5 units

B. 6 units

C. 15 units

D. $\dfrac{5}{\sqrt{3}}$ units

E. 30 units

The correct answer is D.

Triangle XYZ is a 30° - 60° - 90° triangle.

Using the Pythagorean theorem, its sides are therefore in the ratio of $1 : \sqrt{3} : 2$

In other words, using relative measurements, the line segment opposite the 30° angle is 1 unit long, the line segment opposite the 60° angle is $\sqrt{3}$ units long, and the line segment opposite the right angle (the hypotenuse) is 2 units long.

In this problem, line segment XY is opposite the 30° angle, so it is 1 proportional unit long.

Line segment YZ is opposite the 60° angle, so it is $\sqrt{3}$ proportional units long.

Line segment XZ (the hypotenuse) is the angle opposite the right angle, so it is 2 proportional units long.

So, in order to keep the measurements in proportion, we need to set up the following proportion:

$$XY/YZ = 1/\sqrt{3}$$

Now substitute the known measurement of YZ from the above figure, which is 5 in this problem.

$$XY/YZ = 1/\sqrt{3}$$

$$\left(XY/5\right) = 1/\sqrt{3}$$

$$\left(XY/5 \times 5\right) = \left(1/\sqrt{3} \times 5\right)$$

$$XY = 5/\sqrt{3}$$

**Midpoints**

You may be asked to calculate the midpoint of two points on a graph.

Remember that you divide the sum of the two points by 2 because the midpoint is the halfway mark between the two points on the line.

The two points are represented by the coordinates $(x_1, y_1)$ and $(x_2, y_2)$.

The midpoints of two points on a two-dimensional graph are calculated by using the midpoint formula: $(x_1 + x_2) \div 2$ , $(y_1 + y_2) \div 2$

You might see problems like the following one on the exam:

Find the coordinates (x, y) of the midpoint of the line segment on a graph that connects the points (−4, 8) and (2, −6).

However, you may also need to use the midpoint formula in practical problems, like the one that follows.

Problem:

Consider two stores in a town. The first store is a grocery store. The second is a pizza place where customers collect their pizzas after they order them online.

The grocery store is represented by the coordinates (−4, 2) and the pizza place is represented by the coordinates (2,−4).

If the grocery store and the pizza place are connected by a line segment, what is the midpoint of this line?

A. (1, 1)

B. (−1, −1)

C. (2, 2)

D. (−2, −2)

E. (−3, −3)

The correct answer is B.

Remember that to find midpoints, you need to use these formulas:

midpoint $x = (x_1 + x_2) \div 2$

midpoint $y = (y_1 + y_2) \div 2$

First, find the midpoint of the $x$ coordinates for (**−4**, 2) and (**2**,−4).

midpoint $x = (x_1 + x_2) \div 2$

midpoint $x = (−4 + 2) \div 2$

midpoint $x = −2 \div 2$

midpoint $x = −1$

Then find the midpoint of the $y$ coordinates for (−4, **2**) and (2,**−4**).

midpoint $y = (y_1 + y_2) \div 2$

midpoint $y = (2 + -4) \div 2$

midpoint $y = -2 \div 2$

midpoint $y = -1$

So, the midpoint is $(-1, -1)$

**Perimeter of squares and rectangles**

The perimeter is the measurement along the outer side of a square, rectangle, or hybrid shape.

 In order to calculate the perimeter of squares and rectangles, you need to use the perimeter formula, which is provided below.
(length × 2) + (width × 2)

Problem:

What is the perimeter of a rectangle that has a length of 5 and a width of 3?

A. 15

B. 16

C. 18

D. 40

E. 52

The correct answer is B.

Write out the formula.

(length × 2) + (width × 2)

Then substitute the values.

(5 × 2) + (3 × 2)

10 + 6 = 16

## Radians

One radian is the measurement of an angle at the center of a circle which is subtended by an arc that is equal in length to the radius of the circle.

 The radian is equal to 180 ÷ π, which is approximately 57.2958 degrees.

Radians can be illustrated by the diagram and formulas that follow.

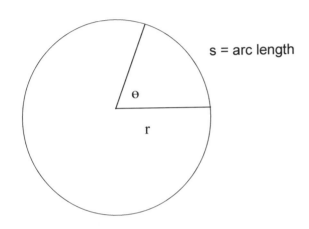 s = arc length

θ = the radians of the subtended angle

s = arc length

r = radius

Accordingly, the following formulas can be used for calculations with radians:

θ = s ÷ r

s = r θ

Also remember these useful formulas.

π × 2 × radian = 360°

π × radian = 180°

π ÷ 2 × radian = 90°

π ÷ 4 × radian = 45°

$\pi \div 6 \times$ radian = 30°

Problem:

If the radius of a circle is 3 and the radians of the subtended angle measure $\pi/3$, what is the length of the arc subtending the central angle?

A. $\pi/3$

B. $\pi/9$

C. $\pi$

D. $3\pi$

E. $9\pi$

The correct answer is C.

We need to use the formula from above to calculate the length of the arc: $s = r\,\theta$

Remember that $\theta$ = the radians of the subtended angle, s = arc length, and r = radius.

So, use the formula from above, and substitute values to solve the problem.

In our problem:

radius (r) = 3

radians ($\theta$) = $\pi/3$

$s = r\,\theta$

$s = 3 \times \pi/3$

$s = \pi$

## Slope and Slope-Intercept

Calculating slope is one of the most important skills that you will need for coordinate geometry problems on the exam.

To put it in simple language, slope is the measurement of how steep a straight line on a graph is.

Slope will be negative when the line slants upwards to the left.

On the other hand, slope will be positive when the line slants upwards to the right.

The two points are represented by the coordinates $(x_1, y_1)$ and $(x_2, y_2)$.

Slope is represented by variable $m$.

We can calculate slope by using the slope formula.

A+ | The slope formula is as follows: $m = \dfrac{y_2 - y_1}{x_2 - x_1}$

You will sometimes be given a set of points, and then told where the line crosses the y axis.

In that case, you will also need what is known as the slope-intercept formula.

In the slope-intercept formula, $m$ is the slope, $b$ is the $y$ intercept (the point at which the line crosses the $y$ axis), and $x$ and $y$ are points on the graph.

A+ | Here is the slope-intercept formula: $y = mx + b$

Problem:

Marta runs up and down a hill near her house. The measurements of the hill can be placed on a two dimensional linear graph on which $x = 5$ and $y = 165$. If the line crosses the $y$ axis at 15, what is the slope of this hill?

A. 10

B. 20

C. 30

D. 36

E. 75

The correct answer is C.

Substitute the values into the formula.

$y = mx + b$

$165 = m5 + 15$

$165 - 15 = m5 + 15 - 15$

$150 = m5$

$150 \div 5 = m5 \div 5$

$30 = m$

**Volume**

The test will have questions that ask you to calculate the volume of certain geometric shapes.

You may need to calculate the volume of a cylinder, cone, or box on the examination.

Box volume: volume = base × width × height
Cone volume: $(\pi \times \text{radius}^2 \times \text{height}) \div 3$
Cylinder volume: $\pi \times \text{radius}^2 \times \text{height}$

Problem 1:

A box is manufactured to contain either laptop computers or notebook computers. When the computer systems are removed from the box, it is reused to hold other items.

If the length of the box is 20cm, the width is 15cm, and the height is 25cm, what is the volume of the box?

A. 150

B. 300

C. 750

D. 7500

E. 15000

The correct answer is D.

To calculate the volume of a box, you need the formula from above:

volume = base × width × height

Now substitute the values from the problem into the formula.

volume = 20 × 15 × 25

volume = 7500

Problem 2:

Consider a cone with a height of 12 inches and a radius at its base of 3 inches. What is the volume of this cone?

A. $3\pi$

B. $12\pi$

C. $36\pi$

D. $72\pi$

E. $108\pi$

The correct answer is C.

Write down the formula.

cone volume = [height × radius$^2$ × π] ÷ 3

Now substitute the values from the problem.

cone volume = [12 × 3$^2$ × π] ÷ 3

cone volume = $36\pi$

## *x* and *y* intercepts

You may also be asked to calculate *x* and *y* intercepts in plane geometry problems.

The *x* intercept is the point at which a line crosses the *x* axis of a graph.

In order for the line to cross the *x* axis, *y* must be equal to zero at that particular point of the graph.

On the other hand, the *y* intercept is the point at which the line crosses the *y* axis.

So, in order for the line to cross the y axis, x must be equal to zero at that particular point of the graph.

For questions about x and y intercepts, substitute 0 for y in the equation provided. Then substitute 0 for x to solve the problem.

Problem:

Find the x and y intercepts of the following equation: $x^2 + 4y^2 = 64$

A. (8, 0) and (0, 4)

B. (0, 8) and (4, 0)

C. (4, 0) and (0, 8)

D. (0, 4) and (8, 0)

E. (0, 0) and (0, 0)

The correct answer is A.

Remember to substitute 0 for y in order to find the x intercept.

$x^2 + 4y^2 = 64$

$x^2 + (4 \times 0) = 64$

$x^2 + 0 = 64$

$x^2 = 64$

$x = 8$

Then substitute 0 for x in order to find the y intercept.

$x^2 + 4y^2 = 64$

$(0 \times 0) + 4y^2 = 64$

$0 + 4y^2 = 64$

$4y^2 \div 4 = 64 \div 4$

$y^2 = 16$

$y = 4$

So, the $y$ intercept is $(0, 4)$ and the $x$ intercept is $(8, 0)$.

## Trigonometry concepts and formulas

Trigonometry questions will evaluate your understanding of the relationships and functions of sine, cosine, and tangent.

Some problems on the test will tell you directly that you need to calculate the sine, cosine, or tangent.

However, the majority of questions on the trigonometry part of the math test will not directly tell you directly which trigonometric function you need to calculate. You will need to evaluate the facts of the problem in order to decide which function you need to use to solve the problem.

For example, the question might show you a triangle and give you the measurements of the degrees of two of the angles in the triangle, and then ask you to calculate the length of one of the sides of the triangle.

More complex problems will show two triangles embedded inside or partially within each other. These are known as hybrid shapes.

In these cases, you will need to use the trigonometry formulas you have learned in order to calculate the degrees or length of one particular part of one of the triangles. Then use that result in another calculation for the second triangle or shape in order to arrive at your final answer.

**Angles**

You will need to understand trigonometric functions in order to calculate angles on the exam.

Remember these important trigonometric formulas:
cos A° = sin (90° − A°)
sin A° = cos (90° − A°)

Problem:

Angles ∠A and ∠B each have measurements between 0° and 45°.

If cos A = sin B, what is the sum of ∠A + ∠B ?

A.  15

B.  30

C.  45

D.  90

E.  180

The correct answer is D.

You will recall from the formulas stated above that:

cos A° = sin (90° − A°)

sin A° = cos (90° − A°)

If sin B = cos A, as in this problem, then B = 90° − A

You can see this more clearly by substituting this value of B into the formula as follows:

A + B = A + (90° − A)

A + B = 90°

**Cosine, sine, and tangent**

Remember the following important trigonometric formulas for calculating the sine, cosine, and tangent of any given angle *A*, as in the illustration that follows.

$\sin A = {}^x/_z$

$\cos A = {}^y/_z$

$\tan A = {}^x/_y$

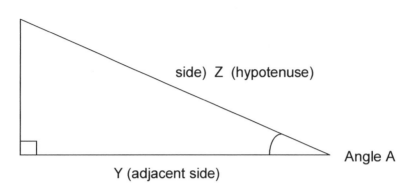

X (opposite                    side)  Z (hypotenuse)

Y (adjacent side)                    Angle A

So, sine is determined by taking the measurement of the opposite side divided by the measurement of the hypotenuse of the triangle.

Cosine is determined by taking the measurement of the adjacent side divided by the measurement of the hypotenuse of the triangle.

Tangent is determined by taking the measurement of the opposite side divided by the measurement of the adjacent side of the triangle.

Memorize these formulas, and then try the problems that follow.

These are the trigonometric relationships for right triangles:

A+

$$\cos^2 A + \sin^2 A = 1$$
$$\cos^2 A = 1 - \sin^2 A$$
$$\sin^2 A = 1 - \cos^2 A$$
$$\tan A = \sin A \div \cos A$$

**Cosine**

Problem 1:

Consider the laws of sines and cosines.

$\cos^2 A = ?$

A. $1 - \sin^2 A$

B. $\sin^2 A - 1$

C. $\tan^2 A$

D. $1 - \tan^2 A$

E. $\tan^2 A - 1$

The correct answer is A.

Remember the formulas stated above. They are valid with respect to any angle, which we refer to here as $A$.

Therefore, $\cos^2$ of any angle is always equal to $1 - \sin^2$ of that angle.

Problem 2:

If $x$ represents a real number, what is the greatest possible value of $4 \times \cos 2x$?

A. 2

B. 3

C. 4

D. 6

E. 12

The correct answer is C.

Remember that the greatest possible value of cosine is 1.

Therefore, $\cos 2x$ must be less than or equal to 1.

So, the greatest possible value of $\cos 2x$ is represented by the following formula:

$\cos 2x = 1$

Now, multiply each side of the equation by 4 in order to get $4 \times \cos 2x$.

$\cos 2x = 1$

$4 \times \cos 2x = 1 \times 4$

$4 \times \cos 2x = 4$

So, the greatest possible value is 4.

**Sine**

Now try these problems in order to practice calculating sine.

Problem 1:

If cos = $\dfrac{10}{26}$ and tan = $\dfrac{24}{10}$ then sin = ?

A. $\sqrt{\dfrac{10}{26}}$

B. $\dfrac{26}{24}$

C. $\dfrac{24}{26}$

D. $\dfrac{24}{10}$

E. $\dfrac{26}{10}$

The correct answer is C.

Remember that for any given angle A:

sin $A = \dfrac{x}{z}$

cos $A = \dfrac{y}{z}$

tan $A = \dfrac{x}{y}$

The facts in our problem stated:

cos = $\dfrac{10}{26}$

$$\tan = \frac{24}{10}$$

So, comparing these facts to the formulas above:

$$\cos A = \frac{y}{z} \text{ and } \tan A = \frac{x}{y}$$

For our problem $\cos = \frac{10}{26}$, so $y = 10$ and $z = 26$

$$\tan = \frac{24}{10}, \text{ so } x = 24 \text{ and } y = 10$$

Now substitute the values for cos.

For our problem, $x = 24$, $y = 10$, and $z = 26$.

$$\sin A = \frac{x}{z}$$

So, in this case $\sin = \frac{24}{26}$

Problem 2:

In the figure below, the length of XZ is 12 units, sin 30° = 0.5, cos 30° = .86603, and tan 30° = 0.57735. Approximately how many units long is XY ?

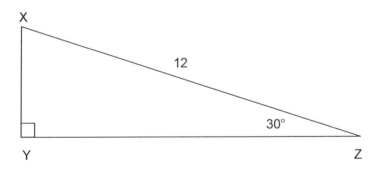

A. 5

B. 5.7735

C. 6

D. 8.6603

E. 36

The correct answer is C.

The sin of angle Z is calculated by dividing XY by XZ.

$\sin z = \frac{XY}{XZ}$

$\sin z = \frac{XY}{12}$

Since angle Z is 30 degrees, we can substitute values as follows:

$\sin z = \frac{XY}{12}$

$0.5 = \frac{XY}{12}$

$0.5 \times 12 = \frac{XY}{12} \times 12$

$0.5 \times 12 = XY$

$6 = XY$

**Tangent**

Problem 1:

If $\cos A = \frac{b}{c}$ and $\sin A = \frac{a}{c}$ then $\tan A = ?$

A. $\frac{c}{a}$

B. $\frac{c}{b}$

C. $\frac{ab}{c}$

D. $\frac{a}{b}$

E. $\frac{b}{a}$

The correct answer is D.

The above question tests your recall of the trigonometric formulas.

Problem 2:

The angle that runs from the treehouse at the top of the tree (T) and the gate in the fence (G) in the Carlson's back yard forms a 70° angle. If the distance between the bottom of the tree (B) and the gate in the fence (G) is 57 feet, what equation below calculates the distance in feet from the treehouse (T) to the bottom of the tree (B)?

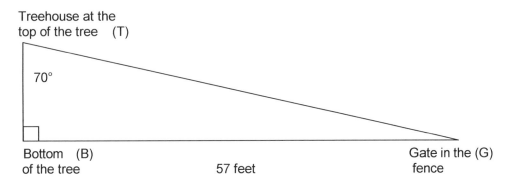

Treehouse at the
top of the tree   (T)

70°

Bottom   (B)
of the tree                        57 feet

Gate in the (G)
fence

A.  $57 \times \tan70°$

B.  $57 \div \tan70°$

C.  $57 \times \cos70°$

D.  $57 \times \sin70°$

E.  $57 \div \sin70°$

The correct answer is B.

Since the three locations form a triangle, the length from the top of the treehouse to the bottom of the tree can be calculated from the tangent of the angle commencing at the treehouse at the top of the tree, which in this case is the tangent of 70°.

$\tan 70° = BG \div TB$

Now substitute the value for line segment BG.

$\tan 70° = 57 \div TB$

Then simplify.

$\tan 70° \times TB = (57 \div TB) \times TB$

$\tan 70° \times TB = 57$

$(\tan 70° \times TB) \div \tan 70° = 57 \div \tan 70°$

$TB = 57 \div \tan 70°$

**ACCUPLACER MATH PRACTICE**

**Arithmetic and Algebra Problems:**

1) 7.23 + .004 + .513 = ?

2) 8.13 × 3.1 = ?

3) Two people are going to give money to a foundation for a project. Person A will provide one-half of the money. Person B will donate one-eighth of the money. What fraction represents the unfunded portion of the project?

4) Which of the following is the least?

A) .32

B) .032

C) .23

D) .302

5) Convert the following to decimal format: $^3/_{20}$

6) 60 is 20 percent of what number?

7) 6¾ − 2½ = ?

8) Estimate the result of the following: 12.9 × 3.1

9) Express 30 percent of *y* as a fraction with 100 as the denominator.

10) 152 ÷ 8 = ?

11) 7.55 + .055 + .02 = ?

12) Estimate the result of the following: 502 ÷ 4.9

13) Beth took a test that had 60 questions. She got 10% of her answers wrong. How many questions did she answer correctly?

14) Which of the following is the greatest?

A) .540

B) .054

C) .045

D) .5045

15) 4.602 − 0.32 = ?

16) 4.27 × 3.1 = ?

17)  A job is shared by 4 workers, A, B, C, and D. Worker A does 1/6 of the total hours. Worker

B does 1/3 of the total hours. Worker C does 1/6 of the total hours. What fraction represents the

remaining hours allocated to person D?

18) 120 students took a math test. The 60 female students in the class had an average score of

95, while the 60 male students in the class had an average of 90. What is the average test

score for all 120 students in the class?

19) $3^1/_2 - 2^2/_5$ = ?

20) .18 ÷ .06 = ?

21) $^1/_{32}$ is equivalent to what percentage?

22) Yesterday the temperature was 90 degrees. Today it is 10% cooler than yesterday.  What is

today's temperature?

23) 1/3 − 1/7 = ?

24) A class contains 20 students. On Tuesday 5% of the students were absent. On Wednesday

20% of the students were absent. How many more students were absent on Wednesday than

on Tuesday?

25) Farmer Brown owns a herd of cattle. This year, his herd consisted of 250 cows. Then he sold 60% of his herd. How many cows did he sell?

26) Estimate the result of the following: $30^{1}/_{4} \times 8^{9}/_{10}$

27) $6.55 \times 1.1 = ?$

28) Three people are going to contribute money to a charity. Person A will provide one-third of the money. Person B will contribute one-half of the money. What fraction represents Person C's contribution of money for the project?

29) The snowfall for November is 5 inches more than for December. If the total snowfall for November and December is 35 inches, what was the snowfall for November?

30) $^{2}/_{3} - ^{1}/_{6} = ?$

31) A museum counts its visitors each day and rounds each daily figure up or down to the nearest 10 people. 104 people visit the museum on Monday, 86 people visit the museum on Tuesday, and 81 people visit the museum on Wednesday. What amount best represents the number of visitors to the museum for the three days, after rounding?

32) Convert the following fraction into decimal format: $^{4}/_{50}$

33) Mount Pleasant is 15,138 feet high. Mount Glacier is 9,927 feet high. What is the best estimate of the difference between the altitudes of the two mountains to the nearest thousand?

34) John is measuring plant growth as part of a botany experiment. Last week, his plant grew 7¾ inches, but this week his plant grew 10½ inches. By how much did this week's growth surpass last week's?

35) At the beginning of a class, one-fourth of the students leave to attend band practice. Later, one half of the remaining students leave to go to PE. If there were 15 students remaining in the class at the end, how many students were in the class at the beginning?

36) $5^1/_3 - 1^1/_4 = ?$

37) $^2/_{10}$ is equivalent to what percentage?

38) Estimate the following: $201 \div 3.9$

39) $1.25 + .655 + .002 = ?$

40) Tom bought a shirt on sale for $12. The original price of the shirt was $15. What was the percentage of the discount on the sale?

41) Shania is entering a talent competition which has three events. The third event (C) counts three times as much as the second event (B), and the second event counts twice as much as the first event (A). What equation, expressed only in terms of variable A, can be used to calculate Shania's final score for the competition?

42) $6 \div 40 = ?$

43) $(-12 + 6) \div 3 = ?$

44) $(x^2 - 4) \div (x + 2) = ?$

45) If $5x - 2(x + 3) = 0$, then $x = ?$

46) Simplify the following equation: $(x + 3y)^2$

47) $(x + 3y)(x - y) = ?$

48) What is the value of the expression $6x^2 - xy + y^2$ when $x = 5$ and $y = -1$ ?

49) Two people are going to work on a job. The first person will be paid $7.25 per hour. The second person will be paid $10.50 per hour. If A represents the number of hours the first person will work, and B represents the number of hours the second person will work, what equation represents the total cost of the wages for this job?

50) If a circle A has a radius of 4, what is the circumference of the circle?

51) $8^7 \times 8^3 = ?$

52) $20 - \frac{3}{4}X > 17$, then $X < ?$

53) –6(4 – 1) – 2(5 – 2) = ?

54) Simplify: | 3 – 6 |

55) Express the following number in scientific notation: 625

56) $\sqrt{5}$ is equivalent to what number in exponential notation?

57) State the $x$ and $y$ intercepts that fall on the straight line represented by the following equation: $y = x + 6$

58) (5$x$ + 7$y$) + (3$x$ – 9$y$) = ?

59) Simplify the following: (5$x^2$ + 3$x$ – 4) – (6$x^2$ – 5$x$ + 8)

60) ($x$ – 4)(3$x$ + 2) = ?

61) Simplify: $\sqrt{7}$ + 2$\sqrt{7}$

62) Factor the following: $x^2$ + $x$ – 20

63) ( –5 – ( –14)) ÷ 2 = ?

64) Mark's final grade for a course is based on the grades from two tests, A and B. Test A counts toward 35% of his final grade. Test B counts toward 65% of his final grade. What equation is used to calculate Mark's final grade for this course?

65) ($x$ – 4$y$)$^2$ = ?

66) If 4$x$ – 3($x$ + 2) = –3, then $x$ = ?

67) ($x^2$ – $x$ – 12) ÷ ($x$ – 4) = ?

68) (3 + –13) ÷ 5 = ?

69) If A represents the number of apples purchased at 20 cents each and B represents the number of bananas purchased at 25 cents each, what equation represents the total value of the purchase?

70) If circle A has a radius of 0.4 and circle B has a radius of 0.2, what is the difference in area between the two circles?

71) What is the value of the expression $2x^2 + 3xy - y^2$ when $x = 3$ and $y = -3$ ?

72) $(x - y)(3x + y) = ?$

73) $\sqrt{2} \times \sqrt{3} = ?$

74) $-3(5 - 2) - 6(4 - 3) = ?$

75) $20 - {}^4/_5X > 16$, then $X < ?$

76) $(-12 + 8) \div 2 = ?$

77) If $7x - 5(x + 1) = -3$, then $x = ?$

78) Simplify: $(x - 2y)(2x - y)$

79) $(2x - y)(x - 3y) = ?$

80) What is the value of the expression $3x^2 - xy + y^2$ when $x = 2$ and $y = -2$ ?

81) If a circle has a radius of 6, what is the circumference of the circle?

82) $20 - {}^1/_4X > 18$, then $X < ?$

83) $-5(3 - 1) - 2(5 - 7) = ?$

84) $3^4 \times 3^3 = ?$

85) $(2x + 5y)^2 = ?$

86) $-2(4 - 1) - 4(3 - 2) = ?$

87) If $5x - 4(x + 2) = -2$, then $x = ?$

88) $(-10 + 1) \div 3 = ?$

89) What is the value of the expression $x^2 - xy + y^2$ when $x = 4$ and $y = -3$ ?

90) If a circle has a diameter of 18, what is the circumference of the circle?

91) If $x - 2(x + 3) = -8$, then $x = ?$

92) Simplify: $(x - y)(x + y)$

93) $\sqrt{8} \times \sqrt{2} = ?$

94) Factor the following: $2xy - 8x^2y + 6y^2x^2$

95) $(x + 3) - (4 - x) = ?$

96) What number is next in this sequence? 2, 4, 8, 16

97) $5^8 \div 5^2 = ?$

98) Simplify the following: $(4x^2 - 5x - 3) - (x^2 + 10x)$

99) A car travels at 60 miles per hour. The car is currently 240 miles from Denver. How long will it take for the car to get to Denver?

**College-Level Math Problems:**

100) How many 3 letter permutations can be made from the following five letter set: F U N K Y?

101) If $x - 1 > 0$ and $y = x - 1$, then $y > ?$

102) What is the determinant of the following matrix: $\begin{bmatrix} j & k \\ m & n \end{bmatrix}$

103) Find the coordinates $(x, y)$ of the midpoint of the line segment on a graph that connects the points $(-5, 3)$ and $(3, -5)$.

104) The price of socks is \$2 per pair and the price of shoes is \$25 per pair. Anna went shopping for socks and shoes, and she paid \$85 in total. In this purchase, she bought 3 pairs of shoes. How many pairs of socks did she buy?

105) Consider a two-dimensional linear graph where $x = 3$ and $y = 14$. The line crosses the $y$ axis at 5. What is the slope of this line?

106) If $5 + 5(3\sqrt{x} + 4) = 55$, then $\sqrt{x} = ?$

107) What ordered pair is a solution to the following system of equations?

$x + y = 11$

$xy = 24$

108) $xi$ and $yi$ are imaginary numbers. $a$ and $b$ are real numbers. When does $xi - a = yi - b$?

109) Consider a right-angled triangle, where side M and side N form the right angle, and side L

is the hypotenuse. If M = 3 and N = 2, what is the length of side L?

110) Express the equation $2^5 = 32$ as a logarithmic function.

111) $x^{-7} = ?$

112) For the following equation, *i* represents an imaginary number. Simplify the equation:

$(2 - 2i) - (4 - 3i)$

113) $\dfrac{5x^3}{4} \times \dfrac{7}{x^2} = ?$

114) $(-3x)(-6x^4) = ?$

115) $\dfrac{x^2 + 8x + 12}{x^2 + 8x + 16} \times \dfrac{x^2 + 4x}{x^2 + 11x + 30} = ?$

116) $\dfrac{3}{x^2 + 2x + 1} + \dfrac{5}{x^2 + x} = ?$

117) $3 = -\dfrac{1}{8}x$, then *x* = ?

118) $\sqrt{4x - 4} = 6$, then *x* = ?

119) Write the slope-intercept equation for the following coordinates: (3,0) and (8,2)

120) 50 ÷ 5 + 36 ÷ 6 = ?

121) Calculate the slope and the *y* intercept: $3x + 5y = 24$

122) $\dfrac{7x + 7}{x} \div \dfrac{4x + 4}{x^2} = ?$

123) What figure should be placed inside the parentheses? $49x^8 = 7x(\ \ )$

124) $(4x^8 + 5x^5 - 7) - (-6x^5 + 5x^8 - 7) = ?$

125) $\dfrac{2}{3x} = \dfrac{?}{9x^2}$

126) Find the lowest common denominator and express as one fraction: $\dfrac{8}{x} + \dfrac{3}{x+2}$

127) $B = \dfrac{1}{3}CD$  Express in the following form: $D =$

128) What are two possible values of $x$ for the following equation?  $6x^2 + 16x + 8 = 0$

129) Simplify: $\dfrac{x^2}{x^{-8}}$

130) If $W = \dfrac{XY}{Z}$, then $Z = ?$

131) Find the volume of a cylinder whose height is 18 and whose radius is 4.  Use 3.14 for $\pi$.

132) $\dfrac{2}{15x} - \dfrac{4}{21x^2} = ?$

133) $A = \dfrac{1}{2}(B+C)d$, if $A = 120$, $B = 13$, $d = 8$, then $C = ?$

134) Perform the operation:  $10ab^5(5ab^7 - 4b^3 - 10a)$

135) The sum of twice a number and 8 less than the number is the same as the difference between $-28$ and the number.  What is the number?

136) Perform the operation.  Then simplify: $\dfrac{z^2 + 7z + 10}{z^2 + 13z + 40} \div \dfrac{z+8}{z^2 + 16z + 64}$

137) Simplify: $\dfrac{x + \dfrac{1}{x}}{\dfrac{1}{x}}$

138) If $\dfrac{3a}{10} + 9 = 12, a = ?$

139) Prepare the slope-intercept formula, using the data from the following table:

| x | 0 | 4 | 8 |
|---|---|---|---|
| y | 5 | 1 | -3 |

140) If $\dfrac{20}{\sqrt{x^2+7}} = 5$, then $x^2 = ?$

141) Express as a rational number: $\sqrt[3]{\dfrac{64}{125}}$

142) In the standard $(x,y)$ plane, what is the distance between $(3,0)$ and $(6,4)$?

143) Give the slope-intercept formula that defines a line which is perpendicular to the line given

by the formula: $y = \dfrac{1}{2}x + 5$

144) What is the value of $a$ when $\dfrac{b^2 - ab + 24}{b - 12} = b - 2?$

145) $125^{-\frac{2}{3}} = ?$

146) If $\dfrac{18}{\sqrt{x^2+4}} = 6$, then $x = ?$

147) What equation defines a line that is parallel to the line given by the following equation:

$y = -0.5x + 5?$

148) Rationalize the denominator: $\sqrt{\dfrac{16}{3}}$

149) What is the product of $(\sqrt{2} - 5\sqrt{5})$ and $(3\sqrt{2} - 4\sqrt{5})?$

150) For all $x \neq 0$ and $y \neq 0$, $\dfrac{4x}{1/xy} = ?$

151) $64^{3/2} = ?$

152) Simplify: $\dfrac{\sqrt{75}}{3} + \dfrac{5\sqrt{5}}{6}$

153) $\dfrac{\sqrt{36}}{3} + 5\dfrac{\sqrt{5}}{9} = ?$

154) $\sqrt{18} + 4\sqrt{75} + 5\sqrt{27} = ?$

155) The Smith family is having lunch in a diner. They buy hot dogs and hamburgers to eat. The hot dogs cost $2.50 each, and the hamburgers cost $4 each. They buy 3 hamburgers. They also buy hot dogs. The total value of their purchase is $22. How many hot dogs did they buy?

156) $(4x^2 + 3x + 5)(6x^2 - 8) = ?$

157) $13^3 \times 13^5 = ?$

158) Factor the following equation: $6xy - 12x^2y - 24y^2x^2$

159) For all positive integers $x$ and $y$, $x - 5 < 0$ and $y < x + 10$, then $y < ?$

160) $\sqrt{4x^8}\,\sqrt{6x^4} = ?$

161) What number is next in the sequence? 7, 14, 21, 28

162) Find the $x$ and $y$ intercepts of the following equation: $4x^2 + 9y^2 = 36$

163) Find the midpoint between the following coordinates: (2, 2) and (4, –6)

164) $- |\, 10 - 17 \,| = ?$

165) $\sqrt{-9} = ?$

166) Find the determinant of the following two–by–two matrix: $\begin{bmatrix} 4 & -1 \\ 3 & -2 \end{bmatrix}$

167) Convert $3^5 = 243$ to the equivalent logarithmic expression.

168) How many 2 letter combinations can be made from the five letter set: A B C D E?

169) Which one of the following is a solution to the following ordered pairs of equations:

$y = -2x - 1$

$y = x - 4$

A) (0, 1)

B) (1, 3)

C) (4, 0)

D) (1, –3)

170) Find the value of the following:

$$\sum_{x=2}^{4} x + 1$$

171) In the standard (x,y) plane, what is the distance between $(3\sqrt{5},0)$ and $(6\sqrt{5},4)$?

172) $\dfrac{a^3/ab}{b/5b^2} = ?$

173) A magician has a bag of colored scarves for a magic trick that he performs. The bag contains 3 blue scarves, 1 red scarf, 5 green scarves, and 2 orange scarves. If the magician removes scarves at random and the first scarf he removes is red, what is the probability that the next scarf will be orange?

174) **Use the chart below to answer the question that follows.**

| X | Y |
|---|---|
| 2 | 4 |
| 4 | 16 |
| 6 | |
| 8 | 64 |
| 10 | 100 |

The chart above shows the mathematical relationship between $X$ and $Y$. What is the value of $Y$ that is missing from the chart?

175) $(x^2 \div y^3)^3 = ?$

176) Find the area of the right triangle whose base is 2 and height is 5.

177) Consider the laws of sines and cosines for any given angle $A$. $\cos^2 A + \sin^2 A = ?$

178) Find the volume of a cone which has a radius of 3 and a height of 4.

179) $2^4 \times 2^2 = ?$

180) The perimeter of a rectangle is 64 meters. If the width were increased by 2 meters and the length were increased by 3 meters, what is the perimeter of the new rectangle?

181) $(-3x^2 + 7x + 2)(x^2 - 5) = ?$

182) $(A^5 \div A^2)^4 = ?$

183) If Д is a special operation defined by $(x$ Д $y) = (2x \div 4y)$ and $(8$ Д $y) = 16$, then $y = ?$

184) How many 3 letter permutations can be made from the four letter set: Z E B A?

185) Consider a right–angled triangle, where side A and side B form the right angle, and side C is the hypotenuse. If A = 5 and B = 3, what is the length of side C?

186) Consider the vertex of an angle at the center of a circle. If the diameter of the circle is 2, and if the angle measures 90 degrees, what is the arc length relating to the angle?

187) Pat wants to put wooden trim around the floor of her family room. Each piece of wood is 1 foot in length. The room is rectangular and is 12 feet long and 10 feet wide. How many pieces of wood does Pat need for the entire perimeter of the room?

188) The Johnson's have decided to remodel their upstairs. They currently have 4 rooms upstairs that measure 10 feet by 10 feet each. When they remodel, they will make one large room that will be 20 feet by 10 feet and two small rooms that will each be 10 feet by 8 feet. The remaining space is to be allocated to a new bathroom. What are the dimensions of the new bathroom?

189) In the figure below, x and y are parallel lines, and line z is a transversal crossing both x and y. Which three angles are equal in measure? (There are two possible answers.)

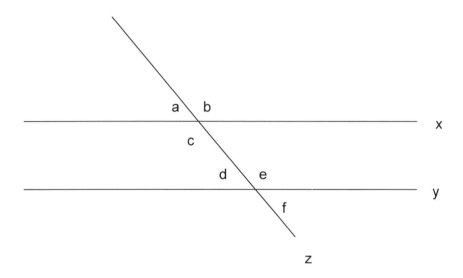

190) The central angle in the circle below measures 45° and is subtended by an arc which is $4\pi$ centimeters in length. How many centimeters long is the radius of this circle?

Arc
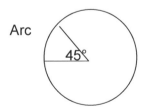

191) In the figure below, XY and WZ are parallel, and lengths are provided in units. What is the area of trapezoid WXYZ in square units?

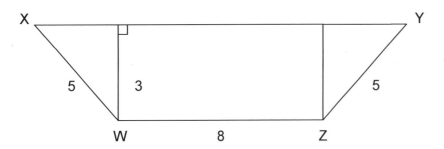

192) In the figure below, the lengths of KL, LM, and KN are provided in units. What is the area of triangle NLM in square units?

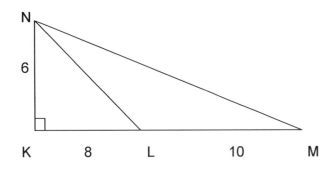

193) ∠XYZ is an isosceles triangle, where XY is equal to YZ. Angle Y is 30° and points W, X, and Z are co−linear. What is the measurement of ∠WXY?

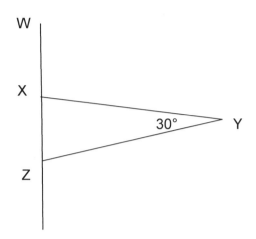

194) Consider the laws of sines and cosines with respect to angle $A$.  $1 - \cos^2 A = ?$

195) If $\cos A = {}^y/_z$ and $\sin A = {}^x/_z$, then $\tan A = ?$

196) In the right triangle below, the length of AC is 5 units and the length of BC is 4 units. What is the tangent of ∠A ?

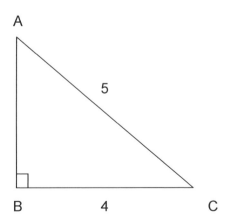

197) In the right angle in the figure below, the length of XZ is 10 units, sin 40° = 0.643, cos 40° = 0.776, and tan 40° = 0.839. Approximately how many units long is XY?

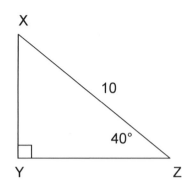

198) An arc length of θ on a circle of radius one subtends an angle of how many radians at the center of the circle?

199) If the radius of a circle is 1, what equation can be used to find the radians in 90°?

200) The street that runs between the hospital (H) and the police station (P) in the illustration below forms a 65° angle. If the police station (P) is 2.5 miles from the fire station (F), what trigonometric equation can be used to calculate the distance of the fire station from the hospital?

H

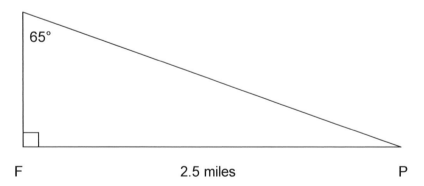

F                2.5 miles               P

**ACCUPLACER MATH PRACTICE – SOLUTIONS AND EXPLANATIONS**

**Solutions to the Arithmetic and Algebra Problems:**

1) The correct answer is: 7.747

When you add on your scratch paper, be sure to line all of the decimals up in a column like this:

7.230
0.004
0.513
7.747

As you can see, you should add zeroes where necessary at the beginning or end of the

numbers in order to make the decimal points line up.

2) The correct answer is: 25.203

Tip: Be sure to put the decimal point in the correct position after you do the long multiplication.

We know that the decimal point has to be three places from the right on the final product

because 8.13 has 2 decimal places and 3.1 has 1 decimal place, so 1 plus 2 equals 3 places.

```
   8.13
×   3.1
   .813
 24.390
 25.203
```

3) The correct answer is: 3/8

The sum of all contributions must be equal to 100%, simplified to 1. Let's say that the variable U

represents the unfunded portion of the project.

So the equation that represents this problem is:  A + B + U = 1

Substitute with the fractions that have been provided: 1/2 + 1/8 + U = 1

Then find the lowest common denominator of the fractions.

4/8 + 1/8 + U = 1

5/8 + U = 1

U = 1 – 5/8

U = 3/8

4) The correct answer is:  0.032

Line all of the decimal points up for problems like this. Put in zeroes where necessary, as

follows:

0.320
0.032
0.230
0.302

When you have them lined up like this, you can see that 0.032 is the smallest one.

5) The correct answer is:  0.15

In order to convert a fraction to a decimal, you must do long division until you have no

remainder.

```
    .15
20)3.00
   2.0
   1.00
   1.00
      0
```

6) The correct answer is: 300

20 percent is equal to 0.20. The phrase "of what number" indicates that we need to divide the

two amounts given in the problem:  $60 \div 0.20 = 300$

We can check this result as follows: $30 \times 0.20 = 60$

7) The correct answer is: 4¼

Questions like this test your knowledge of mixed numbers. Mixed numbers are those that

contain a whole number and a fraction. If the fraction on the first mixed number is greater than

the fraction on the second mixed number, you can subtract the whole numbers and the fractions

separately. Remember to use the lowest common denominator on the fractions.

$6 - 2 = 4$

3/4 − 1/2 = 3/4 − 2/4 = 1/4

Therefore, the result is 4¼.

8) The correct answer is: 39

For estimation problems like this, round the decimals up or down to the nearest whole number.

12.9 is rounded up to 13, and 3.1 is rounded down to 3. Then do long multiplication.

```
   13
×   3
   39
```

9) The correct answer is:  30y/100

This question tests your knowledge of how to express percentages as fractions.

Percentages can always be expressed as that number over one hundred. So 30% = 30/100.

10) The correct answer is: 19

You must do long division until you have no remainder.

```
      19
8) 152
    8
    72
    72
     0
```

11) The correct answer is: 7.625

Remember to line up the decimal points when you add.

```
7.550
0.055
0.020
7.625
```

12) The correct answer is: 100

Remember to round the numbers up or down to the nearest whole number.

502 is rounded down to 500, and 4.9 is rounded up to 5.

Then divide: 500 ÷ 5 = 100

13) The correct answer is: 54

You must first determine the percentage of questions that Beth answered correctly.

We know that she got 10% of the answers wrong, so therefore the remaining 90% were correct.

Now we multiply the total number of questions by the percentage of correct answers.

$60 \times 90\% = 54$

14) The correct answer is: .540

Remember to put in zeroes and line up the decimal points when you compare the numbers.

0.5400

0.0540

0.0450

0.5045

Therefore, the largest number is .540

15) The correct answer: 4.282

Subtract the numbers on your scratch paper, being sure to line the decimals up in a column.

$$\begin{array}{r} 4.602 \\ -0.320 \\ \hline 4.282 \end{array}$$

16) The correct answer is: 13.237

Be careful with the decimal point positions when you do long multiplication.

$$\begin{array}{r} 4.27 \\ \times \quad 3.1 \\ \hline .427 \\ 12.810 \\ \hline 13.237 \end{array}$$

17) The correct answer is: 1/3

The sum of the work from all four people must be equal to 100%, simplified to 1. In other words,

they make up the total hours by working together.

$A + B + C + D = 1$

1/6 + 1/3 + 1/6 + D = 1

Now, find the lowest common denominator of the fractions.

3 × 2 is 6. So the lowest common denominator is 6.

Now convert the fractions as required.

1/3 × 2/2 = 2/6

Now add the fractions together.

1/6 + 2/6 + 1/6 + D = 1

4/6 + D = 1

4/6 − 4/6 + D = 1 − 4/6

D = 1 − 4/6

D = 2/6 = 1/3

18) The correct answer is:  92.5

You need to find the total points for all the females and the total points for all the males.  Then add these two amounts together and divide by the total number of students in the class to get your solution.

Females:  60 × 95 = 5700

Males:  60 × 90 = 5400

(5700 + 5400) ÷ 120 = 11,100 ÷ 120 = 92.5

19) The correct answer is: $1^{1}/_{10}$

Remember that if the fraction on the first mixed number is greater than the fraction on the second mixed number, you can subtract the whole numbers and the fractions separately.

3 − 3 = 1

1/2 − 2/5 = 5/10 − 4/10 = 1/10

Therefore, the result is $1^{1}/_{10}$

20) The correct answer is: 3

You must do long division until you have no remainder. Remember to line up the decimal points.

```
        3.0
.06) .18
     .18
       0
```

21) The correct answer is: 3.125%

$1 \div 32 = 0.03125$

$0.03125 = 3.125\%$

22) The correct answer is: 81 degrees

If it is 10% cooler today, today's temperature is 90% of yesterday's temperature. So today's temperature is 90 degrees × 90% = 81 degrees

23) The correct answer is: $^4/_{21}$

First, find the lowest common denominator.

$^1/_3 \times {}^7/_7 = {}^7/_{21}$

$^1/_7 \times {}^3/_3 = {}^3/{}^{21}$

When you have got both fractions in the same denominator, you subtract them.

$^7/_{21} - {}^3/_{21} = {}^4/_{21}$

24) The correct answer is: 3

Figure out the amount of absences for the two days and then subtract.

Tuesday's absences: 20 × 5% = 1

Wednesday's absences: 20 × 20% = 4

4 − 1 = 3

25) The correct answer is: 150

60% = .60

$250 \times .60 = 150$

26) The correct answer is: 270

Remember to round the fractions up or down to the nearest whole number. Then do the multiplication.

30 × 9 = 270

27) The correct answer is: 7.205

Tip: Be sure to put the decimal point in the correct position after you do the multiplication. You can avoid long multiplication by removing and replacing the decimal points.

Remove the decimal points:

$655 \times 11 = (655 \times 10) + (655 \times 1) =$

6550 + 655 = 7205

6.55 has a decimal point two places from the right. 1.1 has a decimal point 1 place from the right. So we know that we have to put the decimal point *three* numbers from the right on the final product of 7205. Therefore the final answer is 7.205

28) The correct answer is: 1/6

The three people make up the whole contribution by paying in together, so the sum of contributions from all three people must be equal to 100%, simplified to 1.

A + B + C = 1

1/3 + 1/2 + C = 1

Now, find the lowest common denominator of the fractions.

2/6 + 3/6 + C = 1

Therefore, C = 1/6

29) The correct answer is: 20 inches

Subtract the difference in snowfall between the two months from the total snowfall for the two months, and then divide by 2 in order to get the December snowfall.

$35 - 5 = 30$

$30 \div 2 = 15$

Now add back the excess for November to get the total for November.

$15 + 5 = 20$

30) The correct answer is: 1/2

First, find the lowest common denominator.

$2/3 \times 2/2 = 4/6$

When you have got both fractions in the same denominator, you subtract them.

$4/6 - 1/6 = 3/6$, simplified to 1/2

31) The correct answer is: 270

Tip: A basic guideline for rounding is that 5 or more is rounded up, while 4 or less is rounded down.

Do the rounding for each day separately (before doing the addition) because this is stipulated in the problem. Then add together to solve the problem.

104 Rounded to 100

86 Rounded to 90

81 Rounded to 80

$100 + 90 + 80 = 270$

32) The correct answer is: 0.08

Do long division until you have no remainder.

```
     .08
50)4.00
   4.00
      0
```

Alternatively, you know that 50 goes into 100 two times. So you can avoid long division by multiplying the numerator by 2 and adding a decimal point: $4 \times 2 = 8\% = .08$

33) The correct answer is:  5,000 feet

Subtract the two amounts and then do the rounding.  $15,138 - 9,927 = 5,211$ (Rounded to

5,000)

Check by rounding the individual amounts as follows:  $15,000 - 10,000 = 5,000$

34) The correct answer is:  2¾ inches

This is essentially a mixed number problem.  Here you can covert the fraction to decimals to

make the subtraction easier.

$10½ - 7¾ = 10.5 - 7.75 = 2.75 = 2¾$

35) The correct answer is:  40 students

You need to create an equation to set out the facts of this problem.  Here we will say that the

total number of students is variable $S$.

$15 = (S - ¼S) × ½$

$15 = ¾S × ½$

$15 = {}^{3}/_{8}S$

$15 × 8 = {}^{3}/_{8}S × 8$

$120 = 3S$

$S = 40$

36) The correct answer is:  $4{}^{1}/_{12}$

If the fraction on the first mixed number is greater than the fraction on the second mixed

number, you can subtract the whole number and the fractions separately. Remember to use the

lowest common denominator on the fractions.

$5 - 1 = 4$

$1/3 - 1/4 = 4/12 - 3/12 = 1/12$

Therefore, the result is $4{}^{1}/_{12}$.

37) The correct answer is: 20%

2 ÷ 10 = 0.20

0.20 = 20%

38) The correct answer is: 50

Reminder: For estimation problems like this, round the numbers up or down to the nearest whole number.

201 is rounded down to 200, and 3.9 is rounded up to 4. Then divide:  200 ÷ 4 = 50

39) The correct answer is: 1.907

Remember to line up the decimal points as follows:

```
1.250
0.655
0.002
1.907
```

40) The correct answer is: 20%

In order to calculate a discount, you must first determine how much the item was marked down.

$15 − $12 = $3

Then divide the mark down by the original price.

3 ÷ 15 = 0.20

Finally, convert the decimal to a percentage.

0.20 = 20%

41) The correct answer is:  9A

Final Score = A + B + C

B = 2A

C = 3B = 3 × 2A = 6A

Now express the original equation in terms of A:

A + B + C = A + 2A + 6A = 9A

42) The correct answer is: 0.15

Remember to do long division until you have no remainder.

```
      .15
40) 6.00
    4.0
    2.00
    2.00
       0
```

43) The correct answer is: −2

Deal with the part of the equation inside the parentheses first.

$(-12 + 6) \div 3 =$

$-6 \div 3$

Then do the division.

$-6 \div 3 = -2$

44) The correct answer is: $x - 2$

For problems like this, look at the integers in the equation above. In this problem the integers are −4 and 2. We know that we have to divide −4 by 2 because the dividend is $(x + 2)$.

$-4 \div 2 = -2$

We also know that we have to divide $x^2$ by $x$, because these are the first terms in each set of parentheses: $x^2 \div x = x$

Now combine the two parts: $-2 + x = x - 2$

You can check your result as follows: $(x + 2)(x - 2) = x^2 - 2x + 2x - 4 = x^2 - 4$

45) The correct answer is: 2

To solve this type of problem, do multiplication of the items in parentheses first.

$5x - 2(x + 3) = 0$

$5x - 2x - 6 = 0$

Then deal with the integers by putting them on one side of the equation.

$5x - 2x - 6 + 6 = 0 + 6$

$3x = 6$

Then solve for $x$.

$3x = 6$

$x = 6 \div 3$

$x = 2$

46) The correct answer is: $x^2 + 6xy + 9y^2$

$(x + 3y)^2 = (x + 3y)(x + 3y)$

This type of algebraic expression is known as a polynomial. When multiplying polynomials, you should use the FOIL method.

This means that you multiply the terms two at a time from each of the two parts of the equation in this order:

First – Outside – Inside – Last

FIRST: Multiply the first term from the first set of parentheses with the first term from the second set of parentheses.

$x \times x = x^2$

OUTSIDE: Multiply the first term from the first set of parentheses with the second term from the second set of parentheses.

$x \times 3y = 3xy$

INSIDE: Multiply the second term from the first set of parentheses with the first term from the second set of parentheses.

$3y \times x = 3xy$

LAST: Multiply the second term from the first set of parentheses with the second term from the second set of parentheses.

$3y \times 3y = 9y^2$

Then we add all of the above parts together to get:

$x^2 + 3xy + 3xy + 9y^2 =$

$x^2 + 6xy + 9y^2$

47) The correct answer is: $x^2 + 2xy - 3y^2$

Remember to use the FOIL method when you multiply.

FIRST: $x \times x = x^2$

OUTSIDE: $x \times -y = -xy$

INSIDE: $3y \times x = 3xy$

LAST: $3y \times -y = -3y^2$

Then add all of the above once you have completed FOIL.

$x^2 - xy + 3xy - 3y^2 = x^2 + 2xy - 3y^2$

48) The correct answer is: 156

To solve this problem, put in the values for $x$ and $y$ and multiply. Remember to be careful when multiplying negative numbers.

$6x^2 - xy + y^2 =$

$(6 \times 5^2) - (5 \times -1) + (-1^2) =$

$(6 \times 5 \times 5) - (-5) + 1 =$

$(6 \times 25) + 5 + 1 =$

$150 + 5 + 1 =$

156

49) The correct answer is: (7.25A + 10.50B)

The two people are working at different per hour costs, so each person needs to have an individual variable.

A for the number of hours for the first person

B for the number of hours for the second person

So the equation for wages for the first person is: $(7.25 \times A)$

The equation for the wages for the second person is: $(10.50 \times B)$

The total cost of the wages for this job is the sum of the wages of these two people.

$(7.25 \times A) + (10.50 \times B) = (7.25A + 10.50B)$

50) The correct answer is: $8\pi$

The circumference of a circle is always calculated by using this formula.

$\pi$ times the diameter

The diameter of a circle is always equal to the radius times two.

So, the diameter for this circle is $4 \times 2 = 8$. Therefore, the circumference is $8\pi$.

51) The correct answer is: $8^{10}$

This question tests your knowledge of exponent laws. First look to see whether your base number is the same on each part of the equation. (8 is the base number for each part of this equation.)

If the base number is the same, and the problem asks you to multiply, you simply add the exponents.

$8^7 \times 8^3 = 8^{(7+3)} = 8^{10}$

NOTE: If the base number is the same, and the problem asks you to *divide*, you *subtract* the exponents.

52) The correct answer is: 4

In order to solve inequalities, deal with the whole numbers on each side of the equation first.

$20 - \frac{3}{4}X > 17$

$(20 - 20) - \frac{3}{4}X > (17 - 20)$

$-\frac{3}{4}X > -3$

Then deal with the fraction.

$-\frac{3}{4}X > -3$

$4 \times -\frac{3}{4}X > -3 \times 4$

$-3X > -12$

Then deal with the remaining whole numbers.

$-3X > -12$

$-3X \div 3 > -12 \div 3$

$-X > -4$

Then, deal with the negative number.

$-X > -4$

$-X + 4 > -4 + 4$

$-X + 4 > 0$

Finally, isolate the unknown variable as a positive number.

$-X + 4 > 0$

$-X + X + 4 > 0 + X$

$4 > X$

$X < 4$

53) The correct answer is: $-24$

Complete the operations inside the parentheses first.

Remember to be careful when multiplying the negative numbers.

$-6(4 - 1) - 2(5 - 2) =$

$-6(3) - 2(3) =$

$(-6 \times 3) - (2 \times 3) =$

−18 − 6 =

−24

54) The correct answer is: 3

Remember that when you see numbers between lines like this | −3 |, you are being asked the absolute value. Absolute value is always a positive number. So for this question:

| 3 − 6 | = | −3 |

| −3 | = 3

55) The correct answer is: $6.25 \times 10^2$

Scientific notation means that you have to give the number as a multiple of $10^2$, in other words, as a factor of 100.

We know that 625 divided by 100 is 6.25.

So the answer is $6.25 \times 10^2$.

56) The correct answer is: $5^{\frac{1}{2}}$

This question is testing your knowledge of exponent laws. Remember that $\sqrt{x} = x^{\frac{1}{2}}$

57) The correct answer is: (−6, 0) and (0, 6)

To solve problems like this one, begin by substituting 0 for $x$.

$y = x + 6$

$y = 0 + 6$

$y = 6$

Therefore, the coordinates (0, 6) represent the $y$ intercept.

Now substitute 0 for $y$.

$y = x + 6$

$0 = x + 6$

$0 - 6 = x + 6 - 6$

$-6 = x$

So, the coordinates (–6, 0) represent the $x$ intercept.

58) The correct answer is: $8x - 2y$

First perform the operations on the parentheses.

$(5x + 7y) + (3x - 9y) =$

$5x + 7y + 3x - 9y$

Then place the $x$ and $y$ terms together.

$5x + 3x + 7y - 9y$

Finally add or subtract the $x$ and $y$ terms.

$5x + 3x + 7y - 9y =$

$8x - 2y$

59) The correct answer is: $-x^2 + 8x - 12$

Remember to perform the operations on the parentheses first and to be careful with the negatives.

$(5x^2 + 3x - 4) - (6x^2 - 5x + 8) = 5x^2 + 3x - 4 - 6x^2 + 5x - 8$

Then place the $x$ or $y$ terms together.

$5x^2 - 6x^2 + 3x + 5x - 4 - 8$

Finally add or subtract the like terms.

$5x^2 - 6x^2 + 3x + 5x - 4 - 8 = -x^2 + 8x - 12$

60) The correct answer is: $3x^2 - 10x - 8$

Remember to use the FOIL method when you multiply.

FIRST: $x \times 3x = 3x^2$

OUTSIDE: $x \times 2 = 2x$

INSIDE: $-4 \times 3x = -12x$

LAST: $-4 \times 2 = -8$

Then add all of the above once you have completed FOIL.

$3x^2 + 2x + -12x + -8 =$

$3x^2 + 2x - 12x - 8 =$

$3x^2 - 10x - 8$

61) The correct answer is: $3\sqrt{7}$

In order to add square roots like this, you need to add the numbers in front of the square root sign.

$\sqrt{7} + 2\sqrt{7} =$

$1\sqrt{7} + 2\sqrt{7} =$

$3\sqrt{7}$

62) The correct answer is: $(x + 5)(x - 4)$

We know that for any problem like this, the answer will be in the format: $(x + ?)(x - ?)$

We know that we need to have a plus sign in one set of parentheses and a minus sign in the other set of parentheses because 20 is negative, and we can get a negative number in problems like this only if we multiply a negative and a positive.

We also know that the factors of 20 need to be one number different than each other because the middle term is $x$, in other words $1x$. The only factors of twenty that meet this criterion are 4 and 5.

Therefore the answer is $(x + 5)(x - 4)$

63) The correct answer is: 4.5

Perform the operations on the parentheses first.

$(-5 - (-14)) \div 2 =$

$(-5 + 14) \div 2 =$

$9 \div 2$

Then divide: $9 \div 2 = 4.5$

64) The correct answer is: .35A + .65B

The two tests are being given different percentages, so each assignment needs to have its own

variable.

A for test A

B for test B

So the value of test A is .35A

The value of test B is .65B

The final grade is the sum of the values of these two variables:   .35A + .65B

65) The correct answer is: $x^2 - 8xy + 16y^2$

$(x - 4y)^2 = (x - 4y)(x - 4y)$

This is another polynomial problem. When multiplying polynomials, you should use the FOIL

method.

First – Outside – Inside – Last

FIRST: $x \times x = x^2$

OUTSIDE: $x \times -4y = -4xy$

INSIDE: $-4y \times x = -4xy$

LAST: $-4y \times -4y = 16y^2$

Then we add all of the above parts together to get:  $x^2 - 8xy + 16y^2$

66) The correct answer is: 3

To solve this type of problem, do multiplication of the items in parentheses first.

$4x - 3(x + 2) = -3$

$4x - 3x - 6 = -3$

Then deal with the integers by putting them on one side of the equation.

$4x - 3x - 6 + 6 = -3 + 6$

$4x - 3x = 3$

Then solve for $x$.

$4x - 3x = 3$

$x = 3$

67) The correct answer is: $(x + 3)$

In order to solve this type of problem, you must do long division of the polynomial.

$$
\begin{array}{r}
x + 3 \phantom{00} \\
x - 4 \overline{) x^2 - x - 12} \\
\underline{x^2 - 4x} \phantom{0000} \\
3x - 12 \\
\underline{3x - 12} \\
0
\end{array}
$$

68) The correct answer is: –2

Deal with the part of the equation inside the parentheses first.

$(3 + -13) \div 5 =$

$-10 \div 5$

Then do the division.

$-10 \div 5 = -2$

69) The correct answer is: .20A + .25B

Remember that each item needs to have its own variable. A for apples and B for bananas. So

the total value of the apples is .20A and the total value of the bananas is .25B

The total value of the purchase is the sum of the values of these two variables.

.20A + .25B

70) The correct answer is: $0.12\pi$

The area of a circle is always: $\pi$ times the radius squared.

Therefore, the area of circle A is: $0.4^2\pi = 0.16\pi$

The area of circle B is: $0.2^2\pi = 0.04\pi$

To calculate the difference in area between the two circles, we then subtract.

$0.16\pi - 0.04\pi = 0.12\pi$

71) The correct answer is: $-18$

To solve this problem, put in the values for $x$ and $y$ and multiply.

Tip: Remember to be careful when multiplying negative numbers.

$2x^2 + 3xy - y^2 =$

$(2 \times 3^2) + (3 \times 3 \times -3) - (-3^2) =$

$(2 \times 3 \times 3) + (3 \times 3 \times -3) - (-3 \times -3) =$

$(2 \times 9) + (3 \times -9) - (9) =$

$18 + (-27) - 9 =$

$18 - 27 - 9 = -18$

72) The correct answer is: $3x^2 - 2xy - y^2$

FIRST: $x \times 3x = 3x^2$

OUTSIDE: $x \times y = xy$

INSIDE: $-y \times 3x = -3xy$

LAST: $-y \times y = -y^2$

Then add all of the above once you have completed FOIL.

$3x^2 + xy + -3xy + -y^2 =$

$3x^2 + xy - 3xy - y^2 =$

$3x^2 - 2xy - y^2$

73) The correct answer is: $\sqrt{6}$

In order to multiply two square roots, multiply the numbers inside the square roots.

$2 \times 3 = 6$

Then put this result inside a square root symbol for your answer: $\sqrt{6}$

74) The correct answer is: $-15$

Remember to complete the operations inside the parentheses first and to be careful when multiplying the negative numbers.

$-3(5 - 2) - 6(4 - 3) =$

$-3(3) - 6(1) =$

$(-3 \times 3) - (6 \times 1) =$

$-9 - 6 =$

$-15$

75) The correct answer is: $X < 5$

To solve inequalities like this one, deal with the whole numbers on each side of the equation first.

$20 - {}^4/_5 X > 16$

$20 - 20 - {}^4/_5 X > 16 - 20$

$-{}^4/_5 X > -4$

Then deal with the fraction.

$-{}^4/_5 X > -4$

$5 \times -^4/_5X > -4 \times 5$

$-4X > -20$

Then deal with the remaining whole numbers.

Remember that if you are multiplying or dividing by a negative number in any inequality problem, you have to reverse the direction of the inequality symbol.

$-4X > -20$

$-4X \div -4 > -20 \div -4$

$X < 5$

76) The correct answer is: $-2$

Deal with the part of the equation inside the parentheses first: $(-12 + 8) \div 2 = -4 \div 2$

Then do the division: $-4 \div 2 = -2$

77) The correct answer is: 1

Do multiplication of the items in parentheses first.

$7x - 5(x + 1) = -3$

$7x - 5x - 5 = -3$

Then deal with the integers by putting them on one side of the equation.

$7x - 5x - 5 + 5 = -3 + 5$

$7x - 5x = 2$

Then solve for $x$.

$2x = 2$

$x = 1$

78) The correct answer is: $2x^2 - 5xy + 2y^2$

Remember to use the FOIL method when you multiply.

FIRST: $x \times 2x = 2x^2$

OUTSIDE: $x \times -y = -xy$

INSIDE: $-2y \times 2x = -4xy$

LAST: $-2y \times -y = 2y^2$

Then add all of the above once you have completed FOIL.

$2x^2 + -xy + -4xy + 2y^2 =$

$2x^2 - xy - 4xy + 2y^2 =$

$2x^2 - 5xy + 2y^2$

79) The correct answer is: $2x^2 - 7xy + 3y^2$

FIRST: $2x \times x = 2x^2$

OUTSIDE: $2x \times -3y = -6xy$

INSIDE: $-y \times x = -xy$

LAST: $-y \times -3y = 3y^2$

Then add all of the above once you have completed FOIL.

$2x^2 + -6xy + -xy + 3y^2 =$

$2x^2 - 7xy + 3y^2$

80) The correct answer is: 20

Put in the values for $x$ and $y$ and multiply.

$3x^2 - xy + y^2 =$

$(3 \times 2^2) - (2 \times -2) + (-2^2) =$

$(3 \times 2 \times 2) - (2 \times -2) + (-2 \times - 2) =$

$(3 \times 4) - (2 \times -2) + (4) =$

$12 - (-4) + 4 =$

$12 + 4 + 4 = 20$

81) The correct answer is: $12\pi$

The circumference of a circle is always: $\pi \times$ diameter

The diameter for this circle is $6 \times 2 = 12$

Therefore, the circumference is $12\pi$.

82) The correct answer is: 8

For inequalities, deal with the whole numbers on each side of the equation first.

$20 - \frac{1}{4}X > 18$

$(20 - 20) - \frac{1}{4}X > (18 - 20)$

$-\frac{1}{4}X > -2$

Then deal with the fraction.

$-\frac{1}{4}X > -2$

$4 \times -\frac{1}{4}X > -2 \times 4$

$-X > -8$

Then, deal with the negative number.

$-X > -8$

$-X + 8 > -8 + 8$

$-X + 8 > 0$

Finally, isolate the unknown variable as a positive number.

$-X + 8 > 0$

$-X + X + 8 > 0 + X$

$8 > X$

$X < 8$

83) The correct answer is: –6

Remember to complete the operations inside the parentheses first and to be careful when multiplying the negative numbers.

–5(3 – 1) – 2(5 – 7) =

–5(2) – 2(–2) =

(–5 × 2) – (2 × –2) =

–10 + 4 = –6

84) The correct answer is: $3^7$

Remember to add the exponents for multiplication problems like this one.

$3^4 \times 3^3 = 3^{3 + 4} = 3^7$

85) The correct answer is: $4x^2 + 20xy + 25y^2$

$(2x + 5y)^2 = (2x + 5y)(2x + 5y)$

FIRST: $2x \times 2x = 4x^2$

OUTSIDE: $2x \times 5y = 10xy$

INSIDE: $5y \times 2x = 10xy$

LAST: $5y \times 5y = 25y^2$

Then we add all of the above parts together to get: $4x^2 + 20xy + 25y^2$

86) The correct answer is: –10

Complete the subtraction inside the parentheses first. Remember to be careful when multiplying the negative numbers.

–2(4 – 1) – 4(3 – 2) =

–2(3) – 4(1) = –6 – 4 =

–10

87) The correct answer is: 6

$5x - 4(x + 2) = -2$

$5x - 4x - 8 = -2$

$x - 8 = -2$

$x - 8 + 8 = -2 + 8$

$x = 6$

88) The correct answer is: –3

Deal with the part of the equation inside the parentheses first.

$(-10 + 1) \div 3 = -9 \div 3$

Then do the division.

$-9 \div 3 = -3$

89) The correct answer is: 37

Put in the values for $x$ and $y$ and multiply.

$x^2 - xy + y^2 =$

$(4^2) - (4 \times -3) + (-3^2) =$

$(4 \times 4) - (4 \times -3) + (-3 \times -3) =$

$16 - (-12) + (9) =$

$16 + 12 + 9 = 37$

90) The correct answer is: $18\pi$

Circumference = $\pi$ × diameter

91) The correct answer is: 2

To solve this type of problem, do multiplication of the items in parentheses first.

$x - 2(x + 3) = -8$

$x - 2x - 6 = -8$

Then deal with the integers by putting them on one side of the equation.

$x - 2x - 6 + 6 = -8 + 6$

$x - 2x = -2$

Then solve for $x$.

$x - 2x = -2$

$-x = -2$

$x = 2$

92) The correct answer is: $x^2 - y^2$

FIRST: $x \times x = x^2$

OUTSIDE: $x \times y = xy$

INSIDE: $-y \times x = -xy$

LAST: $-y \times y = -y^2$

Then add all of the above once you have completed FOIL.

$x^2 + xy + -xy - y^2 = x^2 - y^2$

93) The correct answer is: $\sqrt{16}$

If you are asked to multiply two square roots, multiply the numbers inside the square roots: $8 \times 2 = 16$

Then put this result inside a square root symbol for your answer: $\sqrt{16}$

94)  The correct answer is: $2xy(1 - 4x + 3xy)$

In order to factor an equation, you must figure out what variables are common to each term of the equation. Let's look at this equation:

$2xy - 8x^2y + 6y^2x^2$

We can see that each term contains $x$. We can also see that each term contains $y$. So, now let's factor out $xy$.

$2xy - 8x^2y + 6y^2x^2 =$

$xy(2 - 8x + 6xy)$

Then, think about integers. We can see that all of the terms inside the parentheses are divisible by 2. Now let's factor out the 2. In order to do this, we divide each term inside the parentheses by 2.

$xy(2 - 8x + 6xy) =$

$2xy(1 - 4x + 3xy)$

95) The correct answer is: $2x - 1$

This question is asking you to simplify the terms in the parentheses. First, you should look to see if there is any subtraction or if any of the numbers are negative. In this problem, the second part of the equation is subtracted. So we need to do the operation on the second set of parentheses first.

$(x + 3) - (4 - x) =$

$x + 3 - 4 + x$

Now simplify for the integers and common variable.

$x + 3 - 4 + x =$

$x + x + 3 - 4 =$

$2x - 1$

96) The correct answer is: 32

For questions like this one, try to find the pattern of relationship between the numbers. Here, we can see that:

$2 \times 2 = 4$

$4 \times 2 = 8$

$8 \times 2 = 16$

In other words, the next number in the sequence is always double the previous number.

Therefore the answer is: $16 \times 2 = 32$

97) The correct answer is: $5^6$

This question tests your knowledge of exponent laws. First look to see whether your base number is the same on each part of the equation. (5 is the base number for each part of this equation.) If the base number is the same, and the problem asks you to divide, you simply subtract the exponents.

$5^8 \div 5^2 = 5^{8-2} = 5^6$

98) The correct answer is: $3x^2 - 15x - 3$

For simplification problems, you should look to see if there is any subtraction or if any of the numbers are negative. In this problem, the second part of the equation is subtracted. So we need to perform the operation on the second set of parentheses first.

$(4x^2 - 5x - 3) - (x^2 + 10x) =$

$(4x^2 - 5x - 3) - x^2 - 10x$

Then we can remove the remaining parentheses.

$(4x^2 - 5x - 3) - x^2 - 10x =$

$4x^2 - 5x - 3 - x^2 - 10x$

Now simplify for the integers and common terms.

$4x^2 - 5x - 3 - x^2 - 10x =$

$4x^2 - x^2 - 5x - 10x - 3 =$

$3x^2 - 15x - 3$

99) The correct answer is: 4 hours

Remember to read questions like this one very carefully. If the car travels at 60 miles an hour and needs to go 240 more miles, we need to divide the miles to travel by the miles per hour.

miles to travel ÷ miles per hour = time remaining

So, if we substitute the values from the question, we get:

240 ÷ 60 = 4

In other words, the total time is 4 hours.

**Solutions to the College-Level Algebra and College-Level Math Problems:**

100) The correct answer is: 60

Permutations are like combinations, except permutations take into account the order of the items in each group. In order to calculate the number of permutations of size $S$ taken from $N$ items, you should use this formula:

$N! \div (N - S)!$

For the question above: $N = 5$ and $S = 3$

$N! \div (N - S)! =$

$(5 \times 4 \times 3 \times 2 \times 1) \div (5 - 3)! =$

$(5 \times 4 \times 3 \times 2) \div 2 =$

$120 \div 2 =$

60

101) The correct answer is: $y > 0$

This is an inequality problem. Notice that both equations contain $x - 1$.

Therefore, we can substitute $y$ for $x - 1$ in the first equation:

$x - 1 > 0$

$x - 1 = y$

$y > 0$

102) The correct answer is: $jn - mk$

In order to find the determinant for a two-by-two matrix, you need to cross multiply and then subtract. So $j$ is multiplied by $n$ and $m$ is multiplied by $k$. Then we subtract the two terms to get the determinant: $jn - mk$

103) The correct answer is: $(-1, -1)$

This question covers coordinate geometry. Remember that in order to find midpoints on a line, you need to use the following formula:

For two points on a graph $(x_1, y_1)$ and $(x_2, y_2)$, the midpoint is:

$(x_1 + x_2) \div 2$ , $(y_1 + y_2) \div 2$

Now calculate for $x$ and $y$.

$(-5 + 3) \div 2 = $ midpoint $x$, $(3 + -5) \div 2 = $ midpoint $y$

$-2 \div 2 = $ midpoint $x$, $-2 \div 2 = $ midpoint $y$

$-1 = $ midpoint $x$, $-1 = $ midpoint $y$

104) The correct answer is: 5 pairs

Let's say that the number of pairs of socks is $S$ and the number of pairs of shoes is $H$.

Now let's make an equation to express the above problem.

$(S \times \$2) + (H \times \$25) = \$85$

We know that the number of pairs of shoes is 3, so let's put that in the equation and solve it.

$(S \times \$2) + (H \times \$25) = \$85$

$(S \times \$2) + (3 \times \$25) = \$85$

$(S \times \$2) + \$75 = \$85$

$(S \times \$2) + 75 - 75 = \$85 - \$75$

$(S \times \$2) = \$10$

$\$2S = \$10$

$\$2S \div 2 = \$10 \div 2$

$S = 5$

105) The correct answer is: 3

In order to calculate the slope of a line, you need this formula:

$y = mx + b$

NOTE: $m$ is the slope and $b$ is the $y$ intercept (the point at which the line crosses the $y$ axis).

Now solve for the numbers given in the problem.

$y = mx + b$

$14 = m3 + 5$

$14 - 5 = m3 + 5 - 5$

$9 = m3$

$9 \div 3 = m$

$3 = m$

106) The correct answer is: 2

In equations that have both integers and square roots, first deal with the integers that are outside the parentheses.

$5 + 5(3\sqrt{x} + 4) = 55$

$5 + 15\sqrt{x} + 20 = 55$

$25 + 15\sqrt{x} = 55$

$25 - 25 + 15\sqrt{x} = 55 - 25$

$15\sqrt{x} = 30$

Then divide.

$15\sqrt{x} = 30$

$(15\sqrt{x}) \div 15 = 30 \div 15$

$\sqrt{x} = 2$

107) The correct answer is: (3, 8)

For questions on systems of equations like this one, you should look at the multiplication equation first. Ask yourself, what are the factors of 24?

We know that 24 is the product of the following:

$1 \times 24 = 24$

$2 \times 12 = 24$

$3 \times 8 = 24$

$4 \times 6 = 24$

Now add each of the two factors together to solve the first equation.

$1 + 24 = 25$

$2 + 12 = 14$

$3 + 8 = 11$

$4 + 6 = 10$

(3, 8) solves both equations. Therefore, it is the correct answer.

108) The correct answer is: $a$ must be equal to $b$ and $xi$ must be equal to $yi$

Two complex numbers are equal if and only if their real parts are equal and their imaginary parts are equal.

109) The correct answer is: $\sqrt{13}$

The length of the hypotenuse is always the square root of the sum of the squares of the other two sides of the triangle.

hypotenuse length L = $\sqrt{M^2 + N^2}$

Now put in the values for the above problem.

L = $\sqrt{M^2 + N^2}$

L = $\sqrt{3^2 + 2^2}$

L = $\sqrt{9 + 4}$

$L = \sqrt{13}$

110) The correct answer is: $5 = \log_2 32$

Logarithmic functions are just another way of expressing exponents. Remember that:

$y^x = Z$ is always the same as $x = \log_y Z$

111) The correct answer is: $1 \div x^7$

Remember that a negative exponent is always equal to 1 divided by the variable with a positive

exponent.

Therefore, $x^{-7} = 1 \div x^7$

112) The correct answer is: $-2 + i$

To solve this type of problem, do the operations on the parentheses first.

$(2 - 2i) - (4 - 3i) = 2 - 2i - 4 + 3i$

Then group the real and imaginary numbers together.

$2 - 2i - 4 + 3i =$

$2 - 4 - 2i + 3i =$

$-2 + i$

113) The correct answer is: $\dfrac{35x}{4}$

To solve this problem, multiply the numerator of the first fraction by the numerator of the second

fraction to calculate the numerator of the new fraction. Then multiply the denominators in order

to get the new denominator.  Then simplify, if possible.

$$\frac{5x^3}{4} \times \frac{7}{x^2} = \frac{35x^3}{4x^2} = \frac{35x}{4}$$

114) The correct answer is: $18x^5$

Remember to multiply the base numbers, add the exponents, and be careful with the negatives.

$$\left(-3x\right)\left(-6x^4\right)=$$

$$-3x^1 \times -6^4 =$$

$$18x^5$$

115) The correct answer is: $\dfrac{x^2 + 2x}{x^2 + 9x + 20}$

Factor the numerators and denominators, then cancel out and re-simplify.

$$\frac{x^2 + 8x + 12}{x^2 + 8x + 16} \times \frac{x^2 + 4x}{x^2 + 11x + 30} =$$

$$\frac{(x+2)(x+6)}{(x+4)(x+4)} \times \frac{x(x+4)}{(x+5)(x+6)} =$$

$$\frac{x(x+2)}{(x+4)(x+5)} =$$

$$\frac{x^2 + 2x}{x^2 + 9x + 20}$$

116) The correct answer is: $\dfrac{8x+5}{x^3 + 2x^2 + x}$

Factor the denominators of each fraction in order to help you find the lowest common

denominator (LCD).  Then re-simplify after you have determined the LCD.

$$\frac{3}{x^2 + 2x + 1} + \frac{5}{x^2 + x} =$$

$$\frac{3}{(x+1)(x+1)} + \frac{5}{x(x+1)} =$$

$$\frac{x}{x} \times \frac{3}{(x+1)(x+1)} + \frac{5}{x(x+1)} \times \frac{(x+1)}{(x+1)} =$$

$$\frac{3x}{x(x+1)(x+1)} + \frac{5x+5}{x(x+1)(x+1)} =$$

$$\frac{8x+5}{x(x+1)(x+1)} =$$

$$\frac{8x+5}{x(x^2+2x+1)} =$$

$$\frac{8x+5}{x^3+2x^2+x}$$

117) The correct answer is: −24

Eliminate the fraction by multiplying both sides of the equation by −8.

$$3 = -\frac{1}{8}x$$

$$3 \times -8 = -\frac{1}{8}x \times -8$$

−24 = x

118) The correct answer is: 10

Square both sides of the equation and then isolate x in order to solve the problem.

$$\sqrt{4x-4} = 6$$

$$\sqrt{4x-4}^2 = 6^2$$

4x − 4 = 36

4x − 4 + 4 = 36 + 4

4x = 40

x = 10

119) The correct answer is: $y = {}^2/_5x - {}^6/_5$

Find the slope, represented by variable m, by putting the stated values into the slope formula.

$$\frac{y_2 - y_1}{x_2 - x_1} = m$$

$$\frac{2-0}{8-3} = \frac{2}{5}$$

Then calculate the *y* intercept, represented by variable *b*, by putting the values for *x*, *y*, and *m* into the slope-intercept formula.

*y* = *mx* – *b*

0 = ($^2/_5$ × 3) – *b*

$^6/_5$ = *b*

Finally, express as the slope-intercept equation, using variables *x* and *y*.

*y* = $^2/_5$*x* – $^6/_5$

120) The correct answer is: 16

This question tests your knowledge of order of operations. Remember to do operations on parentheses first, if any. Then do the exponents, if any. Next, do the multiplication and division (from left to right), and finally the addition and subtraction.

50 ÷ 5 + 36 ÷ 6 =

(50 ÷ 5) + (36 ÷ 6) =

10 + 6 = 16

121) The correct answer is:  *b* = $^{24}/_5$ and *m* = –$^3/_5$

Plug in 0 for *x* in order to calculate *b*, the *y* intercept.

$3x + 5y = 24$

$3 \times 0 + 5y = 24$

$5y = 24$

*y* = $^{24}/_5$

(0, $^{24}/_5$) are the coordinates for the *y* intercept.

Now put in 0 for *y* in order to calculate *x*.

$$3x + 5y = 24$$

$$3x + 5 \times 0 = 24$$

$$3x = 24$$

$$x = 8$$

(8, 0) are the coordinates for the *x* intercept.

Next use the slope formula to calculate the slope. Remember to simplify the fraction as much as possible.

$$\frac{y_2 - y_1}{x_2 - x_1} = m$$

$$\frac{0 - \frac{24}{5}}{8 - 0} = m$$

$$\frac{-\frac{24}{5}}{8} = m$$

$$-\frac{24}{5} \div 8 = m$$

$$-\frac{24}{5} \times \frac{1}{8} = m$$

$$-\frac{24}{40} = m$$

$$-\frac{3 \times 8}{5 \times 8} = m$$

$$-\frac{3}{5} = m$$

122) The correct answer is: $\dfrac{7x}{4}$

Invert and multiply by the second fraction. Cancel out, if possible. Then simplify the resulting fraction in order to get your final result.

$$\frac{7x+7}{x} \div \frac{4x+4}{x^2} =$$

$$\frac{7x+7}{x} \times \frac{x^2}{4x+4} =$$

$$\frac{7(x+1)}{x} \times \frac{x^2}{4(x+1)} =$$

$$\frac{7x^2}{4x} =$$

$$\frac{7x}{4}$$

123) The correct answer is: $7x^7$

This is another exponent problem in a slightly different form. Again, you have to remember the basic principles of factoring and the basic principles of multiplying numbers that have exponents. Remember to multiply base numbers and add exponents.

$$49x^8 = 7x(\ \ )$$

$$7x \times 7x^7 = 49x^8$$

124) The correct answer is: $-x^8 + 11x^5$

Deal with the negative sign in front of the second set of parentheses. Then group like terms together in order to simplify.

$$(4x^8 + 5x^5 - 7) - (-6x^5 + 5x^8 - 7) =$$

$$4x^8 + 5x^5 - 7 + 6x^5 - 5x^8 + 7 =$$

$$4x^8 - 5x^8 + 5x^5 + 6x^5 - 7 + 7 =$$

$$-x^8 + 11x^5$$

125) The correct answer is: $6x$

Compare the denominator of the first fraction with the denominator of the second fraction and divide, if possible, in order to find the common factor: $9x^2 \div 3x = 3x$

Now multiply the numerator on the first fraction by this result in order to get the numerator of the second fraction: $2 \times 3x = 6x$

126) The correct answer is: $\dfrac{11x + 16}{x^2 + 2x}$

The LCD in this problem is $x^2 + 2x$. Remember to multiply the numerator and denominator by the same amounts when converting to the LCD.

$$\frac{8}{x} + \frac{3}{x+2} =$$

$$\frac{8}{x} \times \frac{x+2}{x+2} + \frac{3}{x+2} \times \frac{x}{x} =$$

$$\frac{8x+16}{x^2+2x} + \frac{3x}{x^2+2x} =$$

$$\frac{8x+16+3x}{x^2+2x} =$$

$$\frac{11x+16}{x^2+2x}$$

127) The correct answer is: $\dfrac{3B}{C}$

Isolate $D$ by eliminating the fraction and dividing by $C$.

$$B = \frac{1}{3}CD$$

$$B \times 3 = \frac{1}{3} \times 3CD$$

$$3B = CD$$

$$3B \div C = CD \div C$$

$$\frac{3B}{C} = D$$

128) The correct answer is: $-^2/_3$ and $-2$

Factor the equation and then substitute 0 in each part of the factored equation to get your result.

$$6x^2 + 16x + 8 = 0$$

$(3x + 2)(2x + 4) = 0$

Now substitute 0 for $x$ in the first pair of parentheses.

$(3 \times 0 + 2)(2x + 4) = 0$

$2(2x + 4) = 0$

$4x + 8 = 0$

$x = -2$

Then substitute 0 for $x$ in the second pair of parentheses.

$(3x + 2)(2x + 4) = 0$

$(3x + 2)(2 \times 0 + 4) = 0$

$(3x + 2)4 = 0$

$12x + 8 = 0$

$12x + 8 - 8 = 0 - 8$

$12x = -8$

$x = -^8/_{12}$

$x = -^2/_3$

129) The correct answer is: $x^{10}$

$$\frac{x^2}{x^{-8}} = x^2 \div x^{-8} = x^{2--8} = x^{10}$$

130) The correct answer is: $\dfrac{XY}{W}$

Multiply each side of the equation by $Z$. Then divide by $W$ in order to isolate $Z$.

$$W = \frac{XY}{Z}$$

$$W \times Z = \frac{XY}{Z} \times Z$$

WZ = XY

WZ ÷ W = XY ÷ W

$$Z = \frac{XY}{W}$$

131) The correct answer is: 904.32

The formula for the volume (V) of a cylinder is: $V = \pi r^2 h$

In other words, to calculate the volume of a cylinder you take $\pi$ times the radius squared times the height.

Place the stated values into the equation in order to solve the problem.

$V = \pi r^2 h$

$V = 3.14 \times 4^2 \times 18$

V = 3.14 × 16 × 18

V = 904.32

132) The correct answer is: $\dfrac{14x - 20}{105x^2}$

You will know by now that you need to find the LCD and then perform the operation.

$$\frac{2}{15x} - \frac{4}{21x^2} =$$

$$\frac{2}{15x} \times \frac{7x}{7x} - \frac{4}{21x^2} \times \frac{5}{5} =$$

$$\frac{14x}{105x^2} - \frac{20}{105x^2} =$$

$$\frac{14x - 20}{105x^2}$$

133) The correct answer is: 17

Place the stated values into the equation and perform the operations in order to solve the problem.

$$A = \frac{1}{2}(B + C)d$$

$$120 = \frac{1}{2}(13 + C)8$$

$$120 \div 8 = \frac{1}{2}(13 + C)8 \div 8$$

$$15 = \frac{1}{2}(13 + C)$$

$$15 \times 2 = \frac{1}{2} \times 2(13 + C)$$

$$30 = 13 + C$$

17 = C

134) The correct answer is: $50a^2b^{12} - 40ab^8 - 100a^2b^5$

Step 1: Apply the distributive property of multiplication by multiplying the item in front of the opening parenthesis by each item inside the pair of parentheses.

Step 2: Add up the individual products in order to solve the problem.

$$10ab^5(5ab^7 - 4b^3 - 10a) =$$

$(10ab^5 \times 5ab^7) - (10ab^5 \times 4b^3) - (10ab^5 \times 10a) =$

$50a^2b^{12} - 40ab^8 - 100a^2b^5$

135) The correct answer is: −5

Assign a variable to the mystery number. In this case, we will call the number $x$. Then make an equation based on the information stated in the problem.

twice a number = $2x$

8 less than the number = $x - 8$

the sum of twice a number and 8 less than the number = $2x + x - 8$

the difference between −28 and the number = $-28 - x$

So the equation is: $2x + x - 8 = -28 - x$

Finally, solve the equation for $x$.

$2x + x - 8 = -28 - x$

$2x + x - 8 + 8 = -28 + 8 - x$

$2x + x = -20 - x$

$2x + x + x = -20 - x + x$

$4x = -20$

$x = -5$

136) The correct answer is: $z + 2$

Remember to invert and multiply. Then factor and re-simplify, cancelling out where needed.

$$\frac{z^2 + 7z + 10}{z^2 + 13z + 40} \div \frac{z + 8}{z^2 + 16z + 64} =$$

$$\frac{z^2 + 7z + 10}{z^2 + 13z + 40} \times \frac{z^2 + 16z + 64}{z + 8} =$$

$$\frac{(z+2)(z+5)}{(z+8)(z+5)} \times \frac{(z+8)(z+8)}{z+8} =$$

$$\frac{(z+2)}{1} = z + 2$$

137) The correct answer is: $x^2 + 1$

When you see fractions that have fractions within themselves, remember to treat the denominator as the division sign, and then invert and multiply the fractions as usual.

$$\frac{x + \dfrac{1}{x}}{\dfrac{1}{x}} =$$

$$\left(x + \frac{1}{x}\right) \div \frac{1}{x} =$$

$$\left(x + \frac{1}{x}\right) \times x =$$

$$x^2 + \frac{x}{x} =$$

$x^2 + 1$

138) The correct answer is: 10

Eliminate the integer, then the fraction, and then isolate $a$ in order to solve the problem.

$$\frac{3a}{10} + 9 = 12$$

$$\frac{3a}{10} + 9 - 9 = 12 - 9$$

$$\frac{3a}{10} = 3$$

$$\frac{3a}{10} \times 10 = 3 \times 10$$

$3a = 30$

$a = 10$

139) The correct answer is: $y = -x + 5$

First you need to calculate slope (which is variable $m$ in the slope-intercept equation) using the

slope formula: $\dfrac{y_2 - y_1}{x_2 - x_1}$

Substitute the values for $x$ and $y$ from the table in order to calculate the slope.

$$\frac{y_2 - y_1}{x_2 - x_1} =$$

$$\frac{1 - 5}{4 - 0} =$$

$$\frac{-4}{4} = -1$$

We know from the information provided in the table that the $y$ intercept (which is variable $b$ in

the slope-intercept equation) is 5 because of the coordinates (0, 5).

So we place these values into the slope-intercept formula in order to solve the problem.

$y = mx + b$

$y = -1x + 5$

$y = -x + 5$

140) The correct answer is: 9

Eliminate the fraction and the integer. Then eliminate the radical by squaring both sides of the

equation. Finally, isolate $x$ to solve the problem.

$$\frac{20}{\sqrt{x^2+7}} = 5$$

$$\frac{20}{\sqrt{x^2+7}} \times \sqrt{x^2+7} = 5 \times \sqrt{x^2+7}$$

$$20 = 5\sqrt{x^2+7}$$

$$20 \div 5 = (5\sqrt{x^2+7}) \div 5$$

$$4 = \sqrt{x^2+7}$$

$$4^2 = (\sqrt{x^2+7})^2$$

$$16 = x^2 + 7$$

$$16 - 7 = x^2 + 7 - 7$$

$$9 = x^2$$

Tip: Read these types of problems carefully. Sometimes they will ask you to solve for $x^2$ and other times they will ask you to solve for $x$.

141) The correct answer is: $\frac{4}{5}$

You have to find the cube roots of the numerator and denominator in order to eliminate the radical.

$$\sqrt[3]{\frac{64}{125}} = \sqrt[3]{\frac{4 \times 4 \times 4}{5 \times 5 \times 5}} = \frac{4}{5}$$

142) The correct answer is: 5

Tip: To solve this problem, you need the distance formula.

$$d = \sqrt{(x_2 - x_1)^2 + (y_2 - y_1)^2}$$

$$d = \sqrt{(6-3)^2 + (4-0)^2}$$

$$d = \sqrt{3^2 + 16}$$

$$d = \sqrt{9 + 16}$$

$$d = \sqrt{25}$$

$$d = 5$$

143) The correct answer is: $y = -2x + 5$

Tip: Two lines are perpendicular if the product of their slopes is equal to −1.

Step 1: Calculate the slope. We can see that the slope of the line stated in the problem is ½.

Because the lines are perpendicular, we calculate the slope of the new line with this formula: ½ × $m = -1$

So the slope of the perpendicular line is −2.

Step 2: To solve the problem, put the slope that you calculated in step 1 into the formula given in the problem.

For the given line: $y = \dfrac{1}{2}x + 5$

For the perpendicular line: $y = -2x + 5$

144) The correct answer is: 14

First you need to eliminate the fraction and simplify the result as far as possible. Then remove the common terms and integers in order to isolate $a$ and solve the problem.

$$\frac{b^2 - ab + 24}{b - 12} = b - 2$$

$$\frac{b^2 - ab + 24}{b - 12} \times (b - 12) = (b - 2)(b - 12)$$

$b^2 - ab + 24 = (b - 2)(b - 12)$

$b^2 - ab + 24 = b^2 - 14b + 24$

$b^2 - b^2 - ab + 24 - 24 = b^2 - b^2 - 14b + 24 - 24$

$-ab = -14b$

$a = 14$

145) The correct answer is: $\dfrac{1}{25}$

*Tip 1:* When you see a fraction as an exponent, remember that you need to place the base number

inside the radical sign.  The denominator of the exponent is the n<sup>th</sup> root of the radical, and the

numerator of the fraction becomes the new exponent.  Here is an example: $x^{3/4} = (\sqrt[4]{x})^3$  *Tip 2:*

When you see a negative exponent, you remove the negative sign on the exponent by

expressing the number as a fraction, with 1 as the numerator.  Here is an example: $x^{-6} = \dfrac{1}{x^6}$

So you need to combine these two principles in order to solve the problem.

$$125^{-2/3} = \frac{1}{125^{2/3}} = \frac{1}{\sqrt[3]{125}^2} = \frac{1}{(\sqrt[3]{5 \cdot 5 \cdot 5})^2} = \frac{1}{5^2} = \frac{1}{25}$$

146) The correct answer is: $x = \sqrt{5}$

First you need to eliminate the denominator of the fraction.

$$\frac{18}{\sqrt{x^2 + 4}} = 6$$

$$\frac{18}{\sqrt{x^2 + 4}} \times (\sqrt{x^2 + 4}) = 6 \times (\sqrt{x^2 + 4})$$

$$18 = 6\sqrt{x^2 + 4}$$

Then eliminate the integer in front of the radical.

$$18 = 6\sqrt{x^2 + 4}$$

$$18 \div 6 = (6\sqrt{x^2 + 4}) \div 6$$

$$3 = \sqrt{x^2 + 4}$$

Then square both sides of the equation in order to solve the problem.

$$3 = \sqrt{x^2 + 4}$$

$$3^2 = (\sqrt{x^2 + 4})^2$$

$9 = x^2 + 4$

$9 - 4 = x^2 + 4 - 4$

$5 = x^2$

$$x = \sqrt{5}$$

147) The correct answer is: $y = -0.5x + b$

*Tip 1:* If two lines are parallel, they will have the same slope. So we can use the put the same value for *m* into both equations. *Tip 2:* Note that the parallel lines will have a different *y* intercept.

148) The correct answer is: $\dfrac{4\sqrt{3}}{3}$

"Rationalize" means to remove the square root symbol by performing the necessary mathematical operations.

We remove the square root from the denominator as follows:

$$\sqrt{\frac{16}{3}} = \frac{\sqrt{16}}{\sqrt{3}} = \frac{\sqrt{4 \times 4}}{\sqrt{3}} = \frac{4}{\sqrt{3}} = \frac{4 \times \sqrt{3}}{\sqrt{3} \times \sqrt{3}} = \frac{4\sqrt{3}}{3}$$

149) The correct answer is: $106 - 19\sqrt{10}$

Tip 1: Don't panic when you see the radicals. This is just another type of FOIL problem.

Tip 2: When you multiply radicals, multiply the numbers in front of the radicals and then the numbers inside the radicals. Here is an example: $3\sqrt{3} \times 4\sqrt{2} = 12\sqrt{6}$

Now here is the solution to the problem.

$(\sqrt{2} - 5\sqrt{5})(3\sqrt{2} - 4\sqrt{5}) =$

$(\sqrt{2} \times 3\sqrt{2}) + (\sqrt{2} \times -4\sqrt{5}) + (-5\sqrt{5} \times 3\sqrt{2}) + (-5\sqrt{5} \times -4\sqrt{5}) =$

$(3 \times 2) + (-4\sqrt{10}) + (-15\sqrt{10}) + (20 \times 5) =$

$6 - 4\sqrt{10} - 15\sqrt{10} + 100 =$

$106 - 19\sqrt{10}$

150) The correct answer is: $4x^2y$

When the denominator of a fraction contains another fraction, treat the main fraction as the division sign. Then invert and multiply as usual.

$$\frac{4x}{\frac{1}{xy}} = 4x \div \frac{1}{xy} = 4x \times xy = 4x^2y$$

151) $64^{\frac{3}{2}} = ?$

The correct answer is: 512

Here is some further practice with some concepts we have seen earlier. Remember that when you see a fraction as an exponent, you need to place the base number inside the radical sign. The denominator of the exponent is the n[th] root of the radical, and the numerator of the fraction becomes the new exponent. Here is an example: $x^{\frac{3}{4}} = (\sqrt[4]{x})^3$

You will need to simplify the radical as much as possible.

So for our problem: $64^{\frac{3}{2}} = \sqrt{64}^3 = (\sqrt{8 \times 8})^3 = 8^3 = 512$

152) Simplify: $\dfrac{\sqrt{75}}{3} + \dfrac{5\sqrt{5}}{6}$

The correct answer is: $\dfrac{10\sqrt{3} + 5\sqrt{5}}{6}$

Find the LCD and then perform the operations, including simplification of the radical, in order to solve the problem.

$$\dfrac{\sqrt{75}}{3} + \dfrac{5\sqrt{5}}{6} =$$

$$\dfrac{\sqrt{75}}{3} \times \dfrac{2}{2} + \dfrac{5\sqrt{5}}{6} =$$

$$\dfrac{2\sqrt{75}}{6} + \dfrac{5\sqrt{5}}{6} =$$

$$\dfrac{2\sqrt{75} + 5\sqrt{5}}{6} =$$

$$\dfrac{2\sqrt{25 \times 3} + 5\sqrt{5}}{6} =$$

$$\dfrac{2 \times 5\sqrt{3} + 5\sqrt{5}}{6} =$$

$$\dfrac{10\sqrt{3} + 5\sqrt{5}}{6}$$

153) The correct answer is: $2 + \dfrac{5\sqrt{5}}{9}$

Here it appears that we have a mixed number on the second fraction. However, don't let this confuse you. The basic concepts are the same as in the preceding problem.

$$\dfrac{\sqrt{36}}{3} + 5\dfrac{\sqrt{5}}{9} =$$

$$\frac{\sqrt{36}}{3}+\frac{5\sqrt{5}}{9}=$$

$$\frac{\sqrt{36}}{3}\times\frac{3}{3}+\frac{5\sqrt{5}}{9}=$$

$$\frac{3\sqrt{36}}{9}+\frac{5\sqrt{5}}{9}=$$

$$\frac{3\times6}{9}+\frac{5\sqrt{5}}{9}=$$

$$\frac{18}{9}+\frac{5\sqrt{5}}{9}=$$

$$\frac{18+5\sqrt{5}}{9}=$$

$$2+\frac{5\sqrt{5}}{9}$$

154)  The correct answer is: $3\sqrt{2}+35\sqrt{3}$

Find the squared factors of the amounts inside the radical signs.  Then simplify.

$$\sqrt{18}+4\sqrt{75}+5\sqrt{27}=$$

$$\sqrt{2\times9}+4\sqrt{3\times25}+5\sqrt{3\times9}=$$

$$3\sqrt{2}+(4\times5)\sqrt{3}+(5\times3)\sqrt{3}=$$

$$3\sqrt{2}+20\sqrt{3}+15\sqrt{3}=$$

$$3\sqrt{2}+35\sqrt{3}$$

155) The correct answer: 4 hot dogs

The number of hot dogs is $D$ and the number of hamburgers is $H$.

Here is the equation to express the problem:  $(D \times \$2.50) + (H \times \$4) = \$22$

We know that the number of hamburgers is 3, so put that in the equation and solve it.

$(D \times \$2.50) + (H \times \$4) = \$22$

$(D \times \$2.50) + (3 \times \$4) = \$22$

$(D \times \$2.50) + 12 = \$22$

$(D \times \$2.50) + 12 - 12 = \$22 - 12$

$(D \times \$2.50) = \$10$

$\$2.50 D = \$10$

$\$2.50 D \div \$2.50 = \$10 \div \$2.50$

$D = 4$

156) The correct answer is:  $24x^4 + 18x^3 - 2x^2 - 24x - 40$

Use the distributive property of multiplication, group like terms together, and then simplify.

$(4x^2 + 3x + 5)(6x^2 - 8) =$

$(4x^2 \times 6x^2) + (3x \times 6x^2) + (5 \times 6x^2) + [(4x^2 \times -8) + (3x \times -8) + (5 \times -8)] =$

$24x^4 + 18x^3 + 30x^2 + (-32x^2 + -24x + -40) =$

$24x^4 + 18x^3 + 30x^2 - 32x^2 - 24x - 40 =$

$24x^4 + 18x^3 - 2x^2 - 24x - 40$

157) The correct answer is: $13^8$

If the base number is the same, and the problem asks you to multiply, you add the exponents:

$13^3 \times 13^5 = 13^{3 + 5} = 13^8$

158) The correct answer is: $6xy(1 - 2x - 4xy)$

In order to factor an equation, you must figure out what terms are common to each term of the

equation. Let's factor out $xy$.

$6xy - 12x^2y - 24y^2x^2 =$

*xy*(6 − 12*x* − 24*xy*)

Then, think about integers. We can see that all of the terms inside the parentheses are divisible by 6. Now let's factor out the 6. In order to do this, we divide each term inside the parentheses by 6.

*xy*(6 − 12*x* − 24*xy*) =

6*xy*(1 − 2*x* − 4*xy*)

159) The correct answer is: 15

Our question stated that for all positive integers *x* and *y*: *x* − 5 < 0 and *y* < *x* + 10

*y* < ?

To solve inequalities like this one, you should first solve the equation for *x*.

*x* − 5 < 0

*x* − 5 + 5 < 0 + 5

*x* < 5

Now solve for *y* by replacing *x* with its value.

*y* < *x* + 10

*y* < 5 + 10

*y* < 15

160) The correct answer is: $2x^6\sqrt{6}$

Tip: When the two radicals symbols are together like this, you need to multiply them.

$$\sqrt{4x^8}\sqrt{6x^4} =$$

$$\sqrt{4x^8} \times \sqrt{6x^4} =$$

$$\sqrt{24x^{12}} = \sqrt{4 \times 6} \times \sqrt{x^{12}} = 2\sqrt{6} \times x^{\frac{12}{2}} = 2x^6\sqrt{6}$$

161) The correct answer is: 35

First, find the relationship between each of the numbers given. After looking at the numbers given above, we can see that:

7 + 7 = 14

14 + 7 = 21

21 + 7 = 28

Therefore, we have to add 7 to 28 in order to find the solution.

28 + 7 = 35

162) The correct answer is: (3, 0) and (0, 2)

Remember that for questions about $x$ and $y$ intercepts, you need to substitute 0 for $x$ and $y$ to solve the problem.

Solution for $y$ intercept:

$4x^2 + 9y^2 = 36$

$4(0^2) + 9y^2 = 36$

$0 + 9y^2 = 36$

$9y^2 \div 9 = 36 \div 9$

$y^2 = 4$

$y = 2$

So the $y$ intercept is (0, 2)

Solution for $x$ intercept:

$4x^2 + 9y^2 = 36$

$4x^2 + 9(0^2) = 36$

$4x^2 + 0 = 36$

$4x^2 \div 4 = 36 \div 4$

$x^2 = 9$

$x = 3$

So the $x$ intercept is (3, 0)

163) The correct answer is: (3, −2)

For two points on a graph $(x_1, y_1)$ and $(x_2, y_2)$, the midpoint is: $(x_1 + x_2) \div 2$ , $(y_1 + y_2) \div 2$

Now calculate for $x$ and $y$.

$(2 + 4) \div 2$ = midpoint $x$, $(2 − 6) \div 2$ = midpoint $y$

$6 \div 2$ = midpoint $x$, $−4 \div 2$ = midpoint $y$

$3$ = midpoint $x$, $−2$ = midpoint $y$

164) The correct answer is: −7

When you see numbers between lines like this, you need to determine the absolute value.

Remember that the absolute value is always a positive number.

$− | 10 − 17 | =$

$− | −7 |$

So the absolute value of −7 is 7. But notice the negative sign in front of the absolute value

symbol. Therefore, you finally have to give the negative of the absolute value.

$− | −7 | =$

$− (7) =$

$−7$

165) The correct answer is: 3i

Note that it is not possible to find the square root of a negative number by using real numbers.

Therefore, you will have to use imaginary numbers to solve this problem. Imaginary numbers

are represented by the variable i.

So first determine what the square root of the number would be if the number were positive.

$\sqrt{9} = 3$

Now multiply that result by i.

3 × i = 3i

166) The correct answer is: –5

Tip: To find the determinant for a two-by-two matrix, you need to cross multiply and then subtract.

$$\begin{bmatrix} 4 & -1 \\ 3 & -2 \end{bmatrix}$$

So 4 is multiplied by –2 and 3 is multiplied by –1.

Then we subtract the two terms to get the determinant.

(4 × –2) – (3 × –1) =

–8 – (–3) =

–8 + 3 = –5

167) The correct answer is: $\log_3 243 = 5$

Logarithmic functions are just another way of expressing exponents. Remember that:

$\log_y Z = x$ is always the same as $y^x = Z$

So $3^5 = 243$ is the same as $\log_3 243 = 5$

168) The correct answer is: 10

To determine the number of combinations of $S$ at a time that can be made from a set containing

$N$ items, you need this formula: $(N!) \div [(N - S)! \times S!]$

In the problem above, $S = 2$ and $N = 5$ (because there are five letters in the set).

Now substitute the values for $S$ and $N$.

(5 × 4 × 3 × 2 × 1) ÷ [(5 – 2)! × (2!)] =

(5 × 4 × 3 × 2) ÷ [(3 × 2 × 1) × (2 × 1)] =

$120 ÷ 12 = 10$

169) The correct answer is: (1, −3)

Plug in values for $x$ and $y$ to see if they work for both equations.

Answer choice (D) is the only answer that works for both equations.

If $x = 1$

then for $y = (−2 × 1) − 1$

$y = −2 − 1$

$y = −3$

For the second equation:

$y = x − 4$

$−3 = x − 4$

$−3 + 4 = x − 4 + 4$

$1 = x$

170) The correct answer is:  12

Tip:  When you see the sigma sign like this, you need to perform the operation at the right-hand side of the sigma sign.  In this problem, we perform the operation for $x = 2$, $x = 3$ and $x = 4$ (because 4 is the number at the top).  Then we add these individual products together to get the final result.

For $x = 2$:  $x + 1 = 2 + 1 = 3$

For $x = 3$:  $x + 1 = 3 + 1 = 4$

For $x = 4$:  $x + 1 = 4 + 1 = 5$

$3 + 4 + 5 = 12$

171) The correct answer is: $\sqrt{61}$

For this type of problem, you will need the distance formula.

$$d = \sqrt{(x_2 - x_1)^2 + (y_2 - y_1)^2}$$

$$d = \sqrt{(6\sqrt{5} - 3\sqrt{5})^2 + (4 - 0)^2}$$

$$d = \sqrt{(3\sqrt{5})^2 + 16}$$

$$d = \sqrt{(9 \times 5) + 16}$$

$$d = \sqrt{45 + 16}$$

$$d = \sqrt{61}$$

172) The correct answer is: $5a^2$

Hopefully you will be comfortable with this type of problem at this point.

Treat the main fraction as division by inverting and multiplying. Then simplify.

$$\frac{a^3/ab}{b/5b^2} = a^3/ab \div b/5b^2 = a^3/ab \times 5b^2/b = 5a^3b^2/ab^2 = ab^2(5a^2)/ab^2 = 5a^2$$

173) The correct answer is: 20%

For probability problems, your first step is to calculate how many items there are in total, before any are taken away.

Here we have 3 blue scarves, 1 red scarf, 5 green scarves, and 2 orange scarves, so we have 11 scarves in total.

Then deduct the amount that has been taken away. In this problem, one scarf has been removed, so there are 10 scarves remaining.

Since the scarf that was removed was red, there are 2 orange scarves remaining.

So the probability is expressed as a fraction with the remaining pool as the numerator and the remaining total as the denominator, in other words $^2/_{10}$ in this problem.

Finally we convert this to a percentage: $^2/_{10}$ = 20%

174) The correct answer is: 36

Look at the relationship between $X$ and $Y$ in order to solve the problem. In each case, we can see that $Y = X^2$

So if $X = 6$, $Y = 36$

175) The correct answer is: $x^6/y^9$

Tip: When raising a power to a power, you have to multiply the exponent outside of the parentheses by the exponents inside the parentheses.

$$(x^2 \div y^3)^3 =$$

$$x^6 \div y^9 =$$

$$x^6/y^9$$

176) The correct answer is: 5

To solve this problem, you need the following equation:

Triangle area = (base × height) ÷ 2

Now substitute the amounts for base and height.

area = (2 × 5) ÷ 2 =

10 ÷ 2 =

5

177) The correct answer is: 1

For any given angle, $\sin^2$ is always equal to $1 - \cos^2$. In other words, $\cos^2 + \sin^2 = 1$

178) The correct answer is: $12\pi$

To find the volume of a cone, you need this formula:

Cone volume = ($\pi$ × radius$^2$ × height) ÷ 3

Now substitute the values for base and height.

volume = $(\pi 3^2 \times 4) \div 3 =$

$(\pi 9 \times 4) \div 3 =$

$\pi 36 \div 3 =$

$12\pi$

179) The correct answer is: $2^6$

$2^4 \times 2^2 = 2^{(4 + 2)} = 2^6$

180) The correct answer is: 74 meters

Set up equations for the areas of the rectangles both before and after the change, using W for the width and L for the length. Then, isolate variable W for the width. Finally, solve by expressing variable W in terms of L.

BEFORE:

2L + 2W = 64

2W = 64 − 2L

W = 32 − L

AFTER:

? = 2(L + 3) + 2(W + 2)

? = 2(L + 3) + 2(32 − L + 2)

? = (2L + 6) + 2(34 − L)

? = 2L + 6 + 68 − 2L

? = 6 + 68

? = 74

181) The correct answer is: $-3x^4 + 7x^3 + 17x^2 - 35x - 10$

Change the positions of the sets of parentheses. Multiply the first term from the first set of parentheses by all of the terms in the second set of parentheses. Then multiply the second term from the first set of parentheses by all of the terms in the second set of parentheses. Then simplify.

$(-3x^2 + 7x + 2)(x^2 - 5) =$

$(x^2 - 5)(-3x^2 + 7x + 2) =$

$(x^2 \times -3x^2) + (x^2 \times 7x) + (x^2 \times 2) + (-5 \times -3x^2) + (-5 \times 7x) + (-5 \times 2) =$

$-3x^4 + 7x^3 + 2x^2 + 15x^2 - 35x - 10 =$

$-3x^4 + 7x^3 + 17x^2 - 35x - 10$

182) The correct answer is: $A^{12}$

When taking an exponential number to another exponent, you have to multiply the exponents.

$(A^5 \div A^2)^4 =$

$(A^{5-2})^4 =$

$(A^3)^4 =$

$A^{12}$

183) The correct answer is: 0.25

We have the special operation defined as: $(x \, Д \, y) = (2x \div 4y)$.

First of all, look at the relationship between the left-hand side and the right-hand side of this equation in order to determine which operations you need to perform on any new equation containing the operation Д and variables $x$ and $y$.

In other words, in any new equation:

Operation Д is division.

The number or variable immediately after the opening parenthesis is multiplied by 2.

The number or variable immediately before the closing parenthesis is multiplied by 4.

So, the new equation $(8 \, Д \, y) = 16$ becomes $(2 \times 8) \div (4 \times y) = 16$

Now solve for $(2 \times 8) \div (4 \times y) = 16$

$(2 \times 8) \div (4 \times y) = 16$

$16 \div 4y = 16$

$16 = 16 \times 4y$

$16 = 64y$

$y = 0.25$

184) The correct answer is: 24

Permutations are like combinations, except permutations take into account the order of the items in each group. In order to calculate the number of permutations of size $S$ taken from $N$ items, you should use this formula:

$N! \div (N - S)! =$

For the question above:

$N = 4$ and $S = 3$

$N! \div (N - S)! =$

$(4 \times 3 \times 2 \times 1) \div (4 - 3)! =$

$(4 \times 3 \times 2 \times 1) \div 1 =$

$24 \div 1 = 24$

185) The correct answer is: $\sqrt{34}$

The length of the hypotenuse is always the square root of the sum of the squares of the other two sides of the triangle.

hypotenuse length C = $\sqrt{A^2 + B^2}$

Now put in the values for the above problem.

C = $\sqrt{A^2 + B^2}$

C = $\sqrt{5^2 + 3^2}$

$C = \sqrt{25 + 9}$

$C = \sqrt{34}$

186) The correct answer is: $\pi/2$

To solve this problem, you need these three principles:

(1) Arc length is the distance on the outside (or circumference) of a circle.

(2) The circumference of a circle is always $\pi$ times the diameter.

(3) There are 360 degrees in a circle.

The angle in this problem is 90 degrees.

$360 \div 90 = 4$; In other words, we are dealing with the circumference of 1/4 of the circle.

Given that the circumference of this circle is $2\pi$, and we are dealing only with 1/4 of the circle,

then the arc length for this angle is:

$2\pi \div 4 = \pi/2$

187) The correct answer is: 44

Remember that the perimeter is the measurement along the outside edges of the rectangle or

other area. If the room is 12 feet by ten feet, we need 12 feet $\times$ 2 to finish the long sides of the

room and 10 feet $\times$ 2 to finish the shorter sides of the room.

$(12 \times 2) + (10 \times 2) = 44$

188) The correct answer is: 10 feet by 4 feet

First, we have to calculate the total square footage available. If there are 4 rooms which are 10

by 10 each, we have this equation:

$4 \times (10 \times 10) = 400$ square feet in total

Now calculate the square footage of the new rooms.

$20 \times 10 = 200$

$2$ rooms $\times (10 \times 8) = 160$

$200 + 160 = 360$ total square feet for the new rooms

So the remaining square footage for the bathroom is calculated by taking the total minus the square footage of the new rooms. $400 - 360 = 40$ square feet

Since each existing room is 10 feet long, we know that the new bathroom also needs to be 10 feet long in order to fit in. So the new bathroom is 10 feet by 4 feet.

189) The correct answers are: $\angle a$, $\angle d$, and $\angle f$ are equal and $\angle b$, $\angle c$, and $\angle e$ are also equal.

In problems like this, remember that parallel angles will be equal. So, for example, angles a and d are equal, and angles b and e are equal. Also remember that adjacent angles will be equal when bisected by two parallel lines, as with lines x and y in this problem.

Angles b and c are adjacent, and angles d and f are also adjacent. So, $\angle a$, $\angle d$, and $\angle f$ are equal and $\angle b$, $\angle c$, and $\angle e$ are also equal.

190) The correct answer is: 16

Circumference $= \pi \times$ radius $\times 2$

The angle given in the problem is $45°$. If we divide the total $360°$ in the circle by the $45°$ angle, we have: $360 \div 45 = 8$

So, there are 8 such arcs along this circle. We then have to multiply the number of arcs by the length of each arc to get the circumference of the circle: $8 \times 4\pi = 32\pi$ (circumference)

Then, use the formula for the circumference of the circle.

$32\pi = \pi \times 2 \times$ radius

$32\pi \div 2 = \pi \times 2 \times$ radius $\div 2$

$16\pi = \pi \times$ radius

$16 =$ radius

191) The correct answer is: 36

First, calculate the area of the central rectangle. Remember that the area of a rectangle is length times height: $8 \times 3 = 24$

Using the Pythagorean theorem, we know that the base of each triangle is 4:

$5^2 = 3^2 + base^2$

$25 = 9 + base^2$

$25 - 9 = 9 - 9 + base^2$

$16 = base^2$

$4 = base$

Then calculate the area of each of the triangles on each side of the central rectangle.

Remember that the area of a triangle is base times height divided by 2: $(4 \times 3) \div 2 = 6$

So the total area is the area of the main rectangle plus the area of each of the two triangles:

$24 + 6 + 6 = 36$

192) The correct answer is: 30

Remember that the area of a triangle is base times height divided by 2. First, calculate the area of triangle NKM: $6 \times (8 + 10) \div 2 = 54$

Then, calculate the area of the area of triangle NKL: $(6 \times 8) \div 2 = 24$

The remaining triangle NLM is then calculated by subtracting the area of triangle NKL from triangle NKM: $54 - 24 = 30$

193) The correct answer is: 105°

We know that any straight line is 180°. We also know that the sum of the degrees of the three angles of any triangle is also 180°. The sum of angles X, Y, and Z = 180, so the sum of angle X and angle Z equals 180° − 30° = 150°.

Because the triangle is isosceles, angle X and angle Z are equivalent, so we can divide the remaining degrees by 2 as follows: 150° ÷ 2 = 75°. In other words, angle X and angle Z are each 75°.

Then we need to subtract the degree of the angle ∠XYZ from 180° to get the measurement of ∠WXY: 180° − 75° = 105°

194) The correct answer is: $\text{Sin}^2 A$

For any given angle $A$, $\text{Sin}^2 A$ is always equal to $1 - \cos^2 A$ and $\cos^2 A + \sin^2 A = 1$

195) The correct answer is: x/y

Here are important trigonometric formulas for calculating the sine, cosine, and tangent of any given angle $A$:

$\sin A = x/z$

$\cos A = y/z$

$\tan A = x/y$

196) The correct answer is: 4/3

Using the Pythagorean theorem, we know that:

$AB^2 + BC^2 = AC^2$

$AB^2 + 4^2 = 5^2$

$AB^2 + 16 = 25$

$AB^2 + 16 - 16 = 25 - 16$

$AB^2 = 9$

AB = 3

In this problem, the tangent of angle A is calculated by dividing BC by AB.

So the correct answer is 4 ÷ 3 = 4/3

197) The correct answer is:  6.43

The sin of angle Z is calculated by dividing XY by XZ.

sin z = XY/XZ

sin z = XY/10

Since angle Z is 40 degrees, we can substitute values as follows:

sin z = XY/10

0.643 = XY/10

0.643 × 10 = XY/10 × 10

0.643 × 10 = XY

6.43 = XY

198) The correct answer is:  θ

If the radius is 1, the radians will be equal to the arc length.  So the correct answer is θ.

199) The correct answer is:  π ÷ 2 × radians = 90°

The radian is the angle subtended at the center of a circle by an arc that is equal in length to the

radius of the circle.

Therefore, the radian is equal to 180 ÷ π , which is approximately 57.2958 degrees.

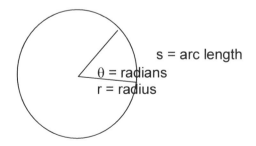

s = arc length

θ = radians

r = radius

The figure above illustrates the calculation of radians. Remember this formula: $\theta = s \div r$

$\theta$ = the radians of the subtended angle

s = arc length

r = radius

Also remember these useful equations:

$\pi \div 6 \times$ radian = 30°

$\pi \div 4 \times$ radian = 45°

$\pi \div 2 \times$ radian = 90°

$\pi \times$ radian = 180°

$\pi \times 2 \times$ radian = 360°

Since this problem contains a 90 degree angle, the answer is the above equation for 90 degrees:  $\pi \div 2 \times$ radians = 90°

200) The correct answer is:  HF = 2.5 ÷ tan 65°

Since the three locations form a triangle, the length from the hospital to the fire station is calculated by taking the tangent of the angle commencing at the hospital, in this case the tangent of 65°.

tan 65° = FP ÷ HF

tan 65° ÷ tan 65° = 2.5 ÷ HF ÷ tan 65°

1 × HF = 2.5 ÷ (HF × HF) ÷ tan 65°

HF = 2.5 ÷ tan 65°

Made in the USA
Lexington, KY
18 April 2014